COGNITIVE YOGA

Mindful Strategies for Teachers

BY

LEE GUERETTE

ISBN: 1490345469
ISBN-13: 9781490345468

REVIEW OF "COGNITIVE YOGA" BY LEE GUERETTE

Lee's writing is an impressive synthesis of the ancient teachings of the Perennial Philosophy and the real-world task of finding unity with complicated students as their schoolteacher. Her personal observations and practical examples and suggestions make reading her book a journey towards heightened empathy and understanding with these children as well as a roadmap of how the classroom situation can be the place of spiritual transformation for the instructor who is open and accepting of the challenge. I would recommend this book even to those who have only to teach themselves, let alone to those brave souls who take on the work of raising each new generation.

Thomas Laage, MD, MPH

Becky Dennison Sakellariou was born and raised in New England and lived much of her adult life in Greece. She is now "making her way home" to New Hampshire to settle for at least half of the year. A teacher and mediator/counselor, she has recently published in <u>*White Pelican Review, Beloit Poetry Journal*</u> and <u>*Common Ground Review*</u>. Nominated for the Pushcart Poetry Prize twice, she also won first prize in the 2005 Blue Light Press Chapbook Contest for her chapbook, *The Importance of Bone*. In 2010, Hobblebush Books of Brookline, NH published her first full-length poetry book, *Earth Listening, and in 2013, her third book, What Shall I Cry?* came out with Finishing Line Press. At present she is madly in love with her three grandchildren and can be found either in Peterborough where she is amazed at the clouds and the colors or in Greece where she putters around on her one acre on the island of Euboia amongst the olive, fig, almond, pomegranate, lemon, apricot and eucalyptus trees

Thank you to Dr. Thomas Laage for his steady encouragement and expertise in Sanskrit and thank you to Becky Sakellariou for her patient and precise work. With gratitude to all my teachers, including the young ones,

LG

Social Emotional Learning is the foundation for all other learning. Teaching students to regulate emotions and work together makes it possible to learn well. From the beginning, the American educational system was seen as the great equalizer so that diverse immigrant populations could learn a common language, break down culture barriers and create literate American citizens. Now the best practices in education have evolved to include the neuroscience of learning and the benefits that result from creating a positive social climate. Educational Leaders have recommended that we move from a presentation of facts and subsequent skill practice to the recognition that subjects must be meaningful, relevant to the community, and that personal engagement is required to learn.

We can no longer afford to be a competitive society where some win at the expense of others. In order to have respect for diversity, and combine their talents, students must understand themselves, empathize with others, and collaborate. S.E.L is the science of creating a transformational environment for our students.

What the world community needs most is: creative solutions to complex problems, ethical personal and social behavior and sustainable systems to save our planet.

C. Lee Guerette

Contact me for a free lecture or more information leeguerette@gmail.com

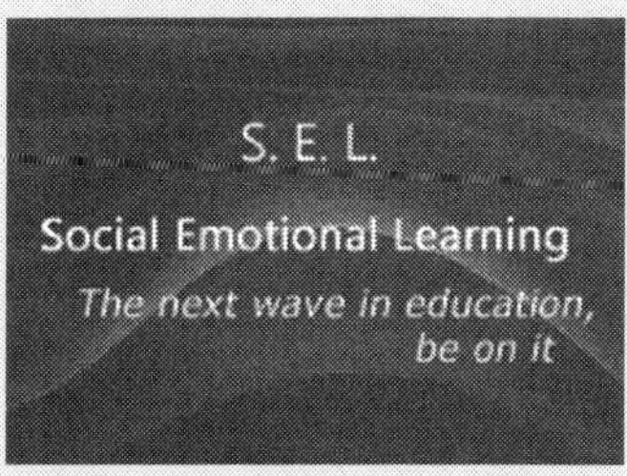

CONTENTS

PREFACE

My hope in writing this book is to help you, the teacher, in two important ways: First, to make your life as a teacher easier. Second, to make your students aware of their ideas and emotions, increase their empathy for other students, and improve their abilities to focus on their work.

I began developing the teaching strategies presented in this book in 1997 after a year working with pre-school children and five years of teaching high school. First I noticed the connection between disruptive classroom behavior and the chaos in students' minds. My struggle to engage them had become plainly apparent. The first chapter of this book describes, in detail, many of my observations during this period.

Classroom control is a necessary condition for teaching; unfortunately, I observed that teachers who appeared to have good control of their classrooms often created this atmosphere through intimidation. I found this personally offensive and set out on a journey to find a more respectful way to get students on task. This book represents the wealth of classroom innovations that I have developed along my way.

Jacqueline, a personal friend and the mother of three children with Attention Deficit Disorder, once offered me a compelling reason for telling her children to obey her. She said that rather than focusing on society's usual explanations for why children must obey their parents, she focused on her belief that ultimately, children must obey themselves. Applying this notion – that we all have to obey ourselves, eventually – is fundamental to the spirit of this book. We need to discriminate between what is useful or not, set a course, and stay on track; no one else fulfills these responsibilities for us. Jacqueline's idea is not unique; in fact, a number of sources have inspired me during this work. For example, I studied Silva Mind Control with Ramona Garcia, took a week long Hypnosis Intensive with Shelley Stockwell-Nicolas and learned from hundreds of other much-loved teachers who shared their wisdom. Just a few of the many books I have read which reflect parts of this philosophy and practice are by Soren Gordhamer, *Just Say Om*, *Meditation for Dummies* by Stephan Bodian, *Life 101* by Peter McWilliams, and the many books by Jon Kabat-Zinn at the University of Massachusetts Medical School.

Most significantly, I have studied these principles over the course of thirty years with my colleagues at the Advaita Meditation Center in Waltham, Massachusetts, an organization that promotes meditation and spiritual inquiry, formerly known as the Philosophy Foundation. Advaita is a spiritual and philosophical tradition of self-realization developed in India and built on the Sringeri approach. The first section of this book, in addition to describing my above-mentioned observations on the connection between students' mental states and their behaviors, also presents fundamental Advaita Vedanta principles that explain the philosophical reasoning that is the foundation for the practices.

The exercises in this book are offered with a demonstration of their spiritual roots; however, most if not all of these techniques can be presented in a secular, scientific way in the classroom. Both common wisdom and scholarly research (*The Neuroscience of Attention, Emotion, & Meditation: Implications for Education* by Alfred W. Kaszniak, Ph.D. and *Mindfulness in the Classroom* by Jon Kabat-Zinn) support the notion that cognitive skills and emotional control improve with stress-reduction techniques.

There are three possible ways for teachers to use these exercises. The first is to offer the strategies as a bag of tricks that might be used to make the classroom better; the second is for the teacher herself to be a practioner but not to directly share the information and insights with the students; and the third is for the teacher to practice diligently, to instruct students only to do what she herself is also doing and to share the adventure with the students. It is not expected that the students learn Vedanata, nor is it necessary for the teacher to become Advaitan. Whatever tradition that is authoritative, has integrity and is found to be personally nourishing, will support you, the teacher, in this work. For the children, it is another step toward freedom, detachment, managing their emotions, and an awareness of their places in this universe.

I

STRUCTURING THE SCHOOL YEAR

CHAPTER 1

MY JOURNEY TO COGNITIVE YOGA

BEGINNINGS

In 1981, I began taking classes at the Practical Philosophy Foundation in Boston. As things unfolded, I noticed that if I followed the instructions, I could concentrate on the task at hand, instead of my usually chaotic mind chattering irrelevant but highly entertaining thoughts. Soon, the efficiency of concentration began to be evident, and I learned that focus actually decreased stress. Eventually, I said to myself, "I can do this at home, too."

The philosophy school was part of a worldwide association of independently run schools that taught the concepts of Advaita Vedanta. In Sanskrit, Advaita means "not two" and Vedanta means "the end of," so Advaita Vedanta may be translated as "the philosophy that ends dualism" or "the philosophy of unity." During the exercises, adult students would discuss a principle such as "focus where the work is taking place" and then practice that with persistence and diligence for an hour or two. During subsequent follow-up class discussion, people would volunteer their observations on moments of clarity or challenges.

Rather than presenting a set of beliefs, the Advaita Meditation Center teaches a way to practice, a practice which leads to experiences, and then those experiences are shared in group discussions. These experiences are compared to and contrasted with the description of moments of enlightenment in classical Hindu texts including the *Upanishads,* the *Gita,* and what other experts have to say about the nature of consciousness. It is important to note that both spirituality and growth towards enlightenment are universal, as opposed to being based on one religion versus another. Ample descriptions of enlightenment are recorded by Christian author, C. S. Lewis, philosopher and Christian mystic, Simone Weil, Transcendentalist poet, Ralph Waldo Emerson, various Catholic saints, and so on.

THE NEXT CHALLENGE

When I began teaching in a middle school in Lowell, Massachusetts in 1997, I had never worked with urban students before, and I didn't understand them. My middle class values were based on taking the Ten Commandments seriously, and I had never met students who believed that because they were "oppressed" by society, they were entitled to lie, cheat, steal, vandalize, break laws, and defy any established authority. Posturing was all about getting power. They formed groups that often substituted for families; for example, they called each other *big brother, baby sister, daddy cakes*, etc. These names signified their feelings and relationships. Their social status in the seventh grade was dependent on how big and bad they could be or how many rules they could break. If they could not dominate or be charismatic enough to lead, then they had to become members of a group that would protect them. School was not in the least bit important when survival was on the line.

In that school, I encountered many students with rough personal stories, and I was really surprised by the way that their personal histories played out in the school environment.

> One student was a Cambodian boy whose mother was socially isolated because she could not speak English. He was a gang member, and she was a "lost soul" in the city. He sat in the back of the room and read the newspaper defiantly. He liked to draw, so I brought in some fine art pens. The pens were stolen the same day.
>
> A 12-year-old girl talked about her unmarried mom going to the emergency room because she had swallowed tongue jewelry and thought the piercing stud might hurt her new boyfriend's unborn baby.
>
> Another child, Roberto, appeared to be daydreaming in the back of the class when he suddenly looked up at me and said, "I'll go to your house and shoot you." Subsequently, the entire class denied that he had said it. Instead of being suspended, he was turned loose in the hallways.
>
> One boy was well off financially because he had inherited money from his father, a drug user, who had died from AIDS. When I had the misfortune of "guessing" that fact, he had a full blow tantrum in class.
>
> A family of five girls, with a drug addicted mother, seldom came to school unless their aunt, who lived in the downstairs apartment and had three children of her own, got them ready and pushed them out the door.

> A six-foot-tall girl threw a book at my head on a whim while I was writing on the board. About 10 years later, I recognized that this girl, now a woman, was working at our city hall, and I asked her through an e-mail if she remember doing that. She claimed absolutely no recall of it.

These students believed that using guns, disrespect for teachers, taking and dealing drugs, stealing, and vandalizing were badges of honor. A thirteen-year-old boy getting stone cold drunk with his Puerto Rican family at a wedding was not even an issue. These students saw "kindness" as weakness, stealing as "cool," and "vulgar insults" as an art form. Although they were precocious about sexual matters, often becoming sexually active as young as 11 or 12, their developmental abilities such as concentration, problem solving, and creativity were delayed. Academically they were frequently two or three years below average in more than one subject.

TURNING ADVERSITY INTO INSPIRATION

I knew by then that I had to do something to get a modicum of control so the students could at least hear the directions for their classroom activities. I also knew firsthand how a thought such as "I'm stupid" or "this is too hard" could derail good opportunities to learn. I had spent 17 years learning how to focus my own attention in spite of distracting or negative thoughts. I dearly wanted to share what I could.

It is worth noting at this point that the movement called "Mindfulness in Education," although rooted in Buddhism, generally presents mindfulness practice for schools, teachers and their students in a secular way. I feel, however, that I have to acknowledge and incorporate the source of the teaching, the over 2000-year old tradition of Advaita Vedanta. Ultimately, Advaita is a way to find peace and happiness. It is taught not by lecture, but rather by *Satanga,* which can be defined as a "dialogue about the nature of reality, trying out a practice and observing the experience that follows."

The word 'Satsanga' is the combination of the two words 'Sat' and 'Sanga.' 'Sat' means existence absolute, which is Brahman. 'Sanga' literally means company or union. To be always in the company of the Lord, or to be established in Brahman, is the literal meaning of the word 'Satsanga.'

Satsanga is association with the wise: Live in the company of sages, saints, Sadhus, Yogis and Sannyasins; hear their valuable Upadesa or instructions; and follow them implicitly. This is Satsanga. (http://hinduism.about.com/od/guru-ssaints/a/satsanga.htm)

Awareness of the mechanics of the mind, emotions, and body has been meticulously investigated by thousands of spiritual teachers and millions of disciples. This book represents my attempt – while embracing the principles of Advaita – to transform this tradition into a practical guide for the classroom environment.

The Stop Exercise (see Chapter 5) was the first practice I implemented in the classroom, and it was somewhat successful. It did give the class a minute of quiet at first. However, when the effectiveness began to wane, I began to give out pencils to the "winner" or quietest child. Some students, usually the most manipulative, would fake "quiet" to get the new pencil, which he or she promptly broke in pencil fights.

After using the Stop Exercise for a few months to begin each class, a moment presented itself when I asked a student – who happened to be overweight – to pull a shade down. The low bookshelf he stepped on to reach the shade collapsed beneath him. This episode could have invited absolute chaos. However, I asked the class to practice the Stop Exercise, and it was the deepest, quietist moment we had shared all year. I then understood that the quality of this moment confirmed my supposition about the potential power of practicing mindfulness techniques in the classroom.

In August of 2000, three years after I used the Stop Exercise in the classroom for the first time, I began teaching at the FW Parker Charter School, which belongs to the Coalition of Essential Schools (CES). The CES schools practice Inquiry Based Learning, and have about 12 students in clusters – called "advisories" – where students are closely monitored by a caring adult teacher. The student population of this school is composed of usually bright, quirky kids from middle-class families who share the values of the essential importance of their children's education. During my time at the Parker Charter School in diverse classroom environments, I built on my experiences, not only from the Stop Exercise, but also other various practices I had learned at the Advaita Meditation Center. Over the course of 10 years, I developed and tried out the most of techniques in this book, and eventually established them as classroom protocols.

HOW TO USE THIS BOOK

In this book, I share the classroom protocols that have emerged from my pedagogical and personal experiences. Most of the chapters present some principle from *Advaita,* a practice and a description of the results. There are also sidebars called "Focus on Students" which contain tips for working with kids with learning disabilities.

As I was taught, I have avoided *telling* my students what they should feel and think, and rather have provided both teacher-scripts and student mental or physical exercises that may promote a sense of calm, unity, benevolence, and/or concentration. One of the tenets of the Coalition of Essential Schools is "to learn to use one's mind well," and a similar Vedanta principle is "the mind is an instrument for my use." It is quite easy to connect those two statements and understand why I believe that the Parker School was the right place to try out these methods. The sequence of the practices, the first nine chapters, are in the order of presentation I used with the students to establish the foundation for the rest of the year. The rest of the techniques are in random order.

The sidebar is a classroom handout that you can copy, give to individual students or post in the room. I have provided some universal ones like the START Exercise but I would encourage you, the teacher, to think about what tasks you want to have the class do regularly. Write the directions, laminate them and create a reference box for common tasks like spelling practice, cleaning out backpacks or writing a composition. Having a handout as a reference will save you time and energy and also decrease potential power struggles which I will discuss further. Throughout the book, you may find footnotes on the Vedanta tenet or source of the practice.

CHAPTER 2

SETTING UP A SERENE CLASSROOM

ETHER, AIR, FIRE, WATER, EARTH

The five elements (or *pancha bhuuta*) are not just Ayurvedic terms, but also more general in the greater scheme of things, as part of the circle of nine points and the constituents of the physical creation. You might think of this as the manifestation of the most subtle, refined substances to the most dense and solid. The proper Sanskrit names are *aakaasha, vaayu, agni, jala*, and *bhuumi* which translate to ether, air, fire, water and earth.

> These elements were prominent and well balanced in my favorite classrooms. The philosophy of *Vastu Shastra* (the Science of Construction) is an ancient Ayurvedic doctrine that describes how to balance and provide proper structure to a home or work place. The theory of this practice is based on directionality, magnetic fields, and the materials of creation. In the context of the classroom,

> I approached it in the simplest, most basic form as my knowledge of this science is quite limited. In spite of that, the atmosphere created by considering these elements was immediate and powerful.
>
> In the resource room where I was to teach Study Skills to all 7th graders, I created a variety of learning centers that invited students to work in small groups or alone. There was a large group table, carrels where students who required no distractions could work, and several niches for students to collaborate in twos and threes. A sunny nook was partitioned off by four-foot high bookshelves that accommodated two rocking chairs, a big leather chair, and a coffee table with floor pillows so that students could spread out their work on the table and kneel or sit close to the floor.

The physical spaces described here balance the five elements of ether, air, fire, water, and earth. Bringing these elements into balance promotes mental clarity and health. Equally important is keeping the work spaces and equipment as clean as possible by wiping down (especially during flu season) door handles, computer keyboards, and anything that is touched or handled frequently.

Furnishing such spaces need not be expensive. Everything needed was acquired as surplus from other classrooms, a used furniture store, and thrift shops. The guiding principle is that the space needs to be welcoming and refined, rather than industrial.

Each of the five parts of the *pancha bhuuta* was represented and reflected in the space.

Ether (*Aakaasha* in Sanskrit) means *emptiness* and is the least dense of the material elements that carries sound. Hard surfaces, such as table tops, increase noise as sound bounces off them, while soft surfaces diminish it. These latter surfaces include cork, quilted fabrics, leafy plants, pillows, rugs, and curtains. Local fire codes often restrict use of these in public buildings, so check into those before acquiring any for your room. Then make sure when setting up tables to create easy access to each and space to walk around them because the notion of Ether/*Aakaasha* is also interpreted to include the flow of classroom traffic. During transitions between classes, a door to "enter" and a door to "exit" keep the river of people from jamming up and creating confusion.

Air *(Vayu)* must be brought into the classroom as much as possible. No matter what the season, regardless of scorching or freezing outdoor temperatures, you need fresh air. Common wisdom tells us that fresh air facilitates an energized mind and body as well as a positive emotional state. Fresh air is also important for another, less obvious reason: it limits the spread of body odor. Older students who use the room often complain about the lingering smells. For all these reasons, if possible, open doors *and windows* to ventilate the room. If the windows are locked, try having lots of plants, a fan and water that mixes into the air by tiny streams or a mister. Fresh air is fundamental to a healthy learning environment.

Fire *(Agni),* although not possible to literally bring into your classroom, can be incorporated through items that imitate fire in various ways. Examples include mirrors, crystals hanging in the sunlight to create rainbows, shiny or reflective surfaces and warm colors. A crystal can serve as a focal point when it is glued just above a whiteboard in the front of the room. Plastic convex mirrors, usually used for blind driveways, enable you to see all the corners of the room. They not only add light, but also provide the additional benefit that all corners of the room are visible without you having to turn around, which cuts back on mischief. That way, when writing notes on the board, you can see behind your back.

Natural light is best, and this can be enhanced in winter by having mirrors on the windowsills that reflect light onto the ceiling or Mylar squares placed on the wall where the sunlight hits. I used to put mirrors facing upward on the windowsills that would reflect sunlight on the ceiling during the cold New England winter afternoons. Most classrooms have fluorescent lighting, which can buzz, flicker, or cast a bluish tint over the room. Plastic covers placed beneath the lights that depict the sky, cherry blossoms, or balloons can perk up fluorescent lights. Full-spectrum table lamps or special bulbs will also improve the atmosphere. By being deliberate with the use of lighting and placement of objects that represent fire like a small mirror ball, you can respect this element without using fire itself.

Water *(Vayu)*, unlike fire, can probably be brought into your classroom by, for example, decorating with a fountain, fish tank, or a scene of the ocean. If you do bring real water into play, it should be kept fresh and moving. You may also find that your usually too-dry room will have some added moisture in it to compensate for the winter heaters. The sound the water makes must be soft and inviting, creating "white noise" that lessens distractions from the hallway. Misters are excellent, but also expensive. Try not to bring in anything the kids would gladly break. Even if you can't bring real water into the learning environment, you may notice a soothing effect on your students (or on you!) when you hear water running or it's raining outside. A background sound of rain on a CD, turned down low, usually has a calming effect.

Earth *(Bhumi)* is all about smell which is the essence of earth and plants. In addition to decorating the classroom with large green leafy plants, I also recommend scented flowers and/or herbs such as mint, rosemary, lemon balm, and gardenia. A large rosemary plant can freshen and change the smell in a room that has been closed for a while. Scented oils in bowls placed in the sunlight also work, but make sure they are in places where they can't be knocked over.

It does not matter whether students know that the elements are balanced in a room in order for it to be effective. People usually feel refreshed in such spaces because the balance of the five elements supports peace and concentration and entices students to work together, read quietly, or collaborate on a project. A good plan for sound management, traffic flow, light, air quality, water, and scent will have a pervasive impact on you and your students. Students should be able to move around the room easily and get supplies independently. A well-balanced room promotes efficiency and frees the teacher to act as a facilitator rather than the lead performer. The time and energy saved can go into paying attention to students.

CHAPTER 3

ELEMENTS OF THE MIND

The organs of the mind, according to Vedanta, are *Buddhi, Chitta, Manas,* and *Ahankara.* The mental/emotional set up as a whole is known as the *Antahkarana.* Some disagree-ment exists amongst scholars as to the exact meaning of these words because of the complex, reflective nature of the Sanskrit language. The translations discussed here are based on my 30 years of studies at the Advaita Meditation Center. For other more detailed interpretations, see **[http://www.hindupedia.com/en/Consciousness_in_Advaita_Vedanta citations]**.

BUDDHI

Under my teachers, I was taught that *Buddhi* means "reason," intellect or discrimination and is one of the organs of the mind. It is used here to mean "insight," and it is unlike what Westerners typically see as reason. Rather than an attempt to come to a solution by thinking of possible directions, *Buddhi* presents a plan, concept or solution as an immediate, clean, clear image. It is the "aha" moment where the solution has to be both intelligent and loving. It is usually preceded by a calm moment when the ego is not pushing for favoritism. The *Buddhi's* informa-tion often comes in a "flash" appearing as a fully formed plan. This kind of reason depends on whether the person asking the question has a clear and unselfish conscious-ness. It usually presents itself as the right course of action to resolve a conflict between two seemingly opposing points of view.

If the person's ego begins to influence an idea with questions about what other people will think of him/her, it is probably *Manas* rather than *Buddhi* that is operating. This is really thinking outside of the box. If the word box can be substituted for "ego," then *Buddhi* arises from a universal consciousness which appears to be a source of limitless creativity. It is fairly rare for this kind of reason to be in play.

MANAS

Manas is the active chattering that usually goes on in the mind. A well-trained *Manas* will present ideas and possible scenarios to address situations, but it is ego driven and more often than not comes from memory and experiences. *Manas* is a useful tool, but it represents a review of known facts in memory. *Manas* has been called "monkey mind" because it is often disobedient and willful. If anything "just wants to have fun," it is *Manas. Manas* is also the organ of mind that produces repetitive, or "circling" thoughts, like worry, criticism or desire. Side-stepping *Manas* means deliberate observation in real time often supported by connecting to the senses. *Be here, Be now.*

CHITTA

Chitta, as the terminology is used at the Advaita Meditation Center, is the "emotional attitude" or "heart" of the individual. You may know people who are pervasively "cheerful and hardworking" and others who always seem "defeated." Unlike moods and emotions, the qualities of *Chitta* are more indicative of personality traits than they are of temporary states of being. It is worth noting that successful learning interventions work "with" rather than against a student's deeply held way of being in this world. A child who is slow and careful is unlikely to change to a quick and perfunctory mode for a particular task, so if you are in charge of a group project, consider who is likely to be successful in a particular role. Our heart - *Chitta* - contributes our special influence on creation. The configuration of energy that is what we love, study, and do well authentically, is our gift to this world.

BHĀVANĀ

This Sanskrit word holds the essential idea of bringing into creation or being drawn to that which you love. If you want to motivate students, offer them a taste of what they love, a cause or reason to complete an action that will inspire them to create with gusto. When students did their "activism" projects at the Parker, they created posters, raised money, and created songs related to their favorite charity. These presentations were about topics that were important to them personally such as prevention of cruelty to animals, feeding the poor, supplying school materials to students in Africa. The passion that they feel for a righteous cause is what pushes them to manifest a high quality material representation of their ideas.

AHAṀKĀRA

Lastly, *Ahankara* is the organ of mind that is the equivalent to the ego or "doer." *Ahankara* is the collection of ideas that we have about ourselves. It is often described as an individual's lists of likes and dislikes which emerge from subjective opinions. Sometimes *Ahankara* creates habitual fears and aversions. These ideas are not real in a permanent sense, but they are stubborn impressions and require lots of purification of mind to dismiss. Usually the *Ahankara* sees itself as a hero or a victim in the narrative of his/her life. We create our identity with the trends and patterns of *Ahankara*, but it is a limited, false, self. The *Ahankara* struggles to preserve a sense of me, myself, my stuff, my story, basically to prove to itself that it is important and real. Vedanta holds that this idea of a separate individual, a personal and limited identity, is our master illusion. *Brahman* seeks to know himself by becoming and experiencing all. But in essence, all is *Brahman* only.

The purpose of giving you the above terms is that you can use them to understand what is operative in the child's mind. *Manas* is often head chatter, *Chitta* may be a pervasive attitude, or *Ahankara* may be a habitual thought that prevents a child from making a sincere effort. Your ability to understand these **mechanics** of the mind will support teaching in an effective way.

When there is an opportunity to work quietly with a child, the teacher may observe the student's mental process by asking questions about how s/he approaches her/his work. You might ask if the task feels "overwhelming," which indicates a discouraged *Ahankara*. If the student appears to be distracted by irrelevant ideas and thoughts, this indicates *Manas*. These concepts help refine your language and intuitions about the child's learning challenges.

The objective when working with a child is to work with her/his current state, accept it and offer a step toward more freedom. For example, a child with a learning disability may adopt an attitude of "helplessness" or "I can't make myself learn that because I am flawed, defective or special." Their "specialness" might hamper a full, sincere effort to try something new. The teacher should suggest that other, previous challenges have been overcome which show that the student is capable. Tell the student to trust that when different strategies are tried, he/she will know what works for them. Keeping

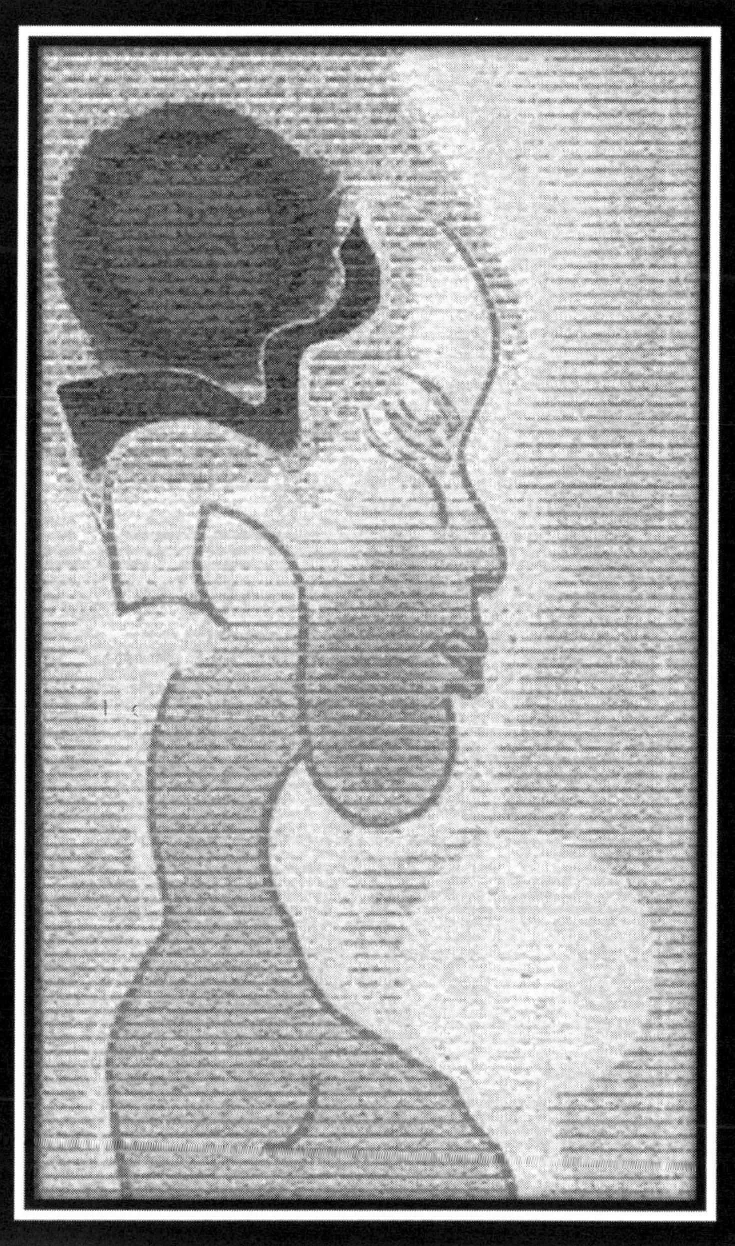

them curious, confident and an observer of their own mental processes will support the fearlessness required to take on difficulties.

People do not decide themselves when they are born that they will collect a cluster of ideas, attitudes, and emotions that will make it hard for them to concentrate or learn. However, the mechanical nature of the mind appears to create impediments that require examination and release. Whenever a person becomes more still, these ideas rise up in opposition as the person's determination to pay attention increases. When you observe your students' behavior, if you are able to recognize the process that is happening and the specific nature of the block – whether it is an idea, an emotion, head chatter, or identification as the doer – you will be better equipped to talk about the block with compassion and understanding.

CHAPTER 4

GREETING STUDENTS

It important that the teacher set the tone for the class from the beginning. Tone, metaphorically, is the sound of your own heart, your core attitude. From day one, establish an invitation towards a sense of mutual respect and intention to do hard work in this place. Your sense of groundedness and stability is supported by your own meditation.

There are three basic way to use this information. The first is for the teacher to practice regular meditation her/himself and have that as a source of resilience. The second is to use the techniques as a classroom management strategy without personal practice. The third to have both, a teacher who is grounded in meditation and her/his own practice who presents the strategies to the group and honors the student's experiences.

It is no simple thing to establish appropriate boundaries. Think about a Sensei, a Karate master; s/he may stand calmly in front of the class but there is no doubt that she/he could throw you on the floor if desired. It isn't the use of force that sets the boundary, it is the belief that if a boundary is crossed, the consequence will be fair, certain and swift. Hopefully, in your school, discipline is effective, but with many students, a lack of parental supervision and the middle-schooler's abundant energy make teaching feel like keeping a cover on a boiling pot. If the students are allowed to come in and begin their own chatter before you set up the lesson, a great deal of time and energy can be used trying to get their attention focused.

You may want to try greeting them at the door as they come in and say the directions for the day for each student. Like this: "Good morning, Maria, we are going to be doing some Latin and Greek roots today. This is your packet." Give them a sheet with the directions. "Please sit down there (point to a designated seat) and begin your work silently for the next few minutes." If the child does not look you in the eye or refuses to comply, call him/her back and repeat the process until you get some assent. You can also greet them standing up in the front of the classroom. The stronger method is one by one with a handshake and a direct look in the eye if possible. A group cannot be disciplined as a whole. Discipline is done one by one, preferably privately.

Focus on Students

Most young people are acutely aware of others because the parts of the brain that interpret body language, tone and peer pressure are functioning well. Students on the autism scale, however, do not process emotions this way. If they are on the N.L.D. spectrum, they do not become motivated by external factors. Punishment, rewards, peer pressure, and so on, do not persuade them. However, connections to topics that are already of interest and extensions to those topics frequently entice them.

You will know which ones will be obstinate if they try to dance around you, avoid eye contact and generally try to hustle the room. Sometimes the students tune out the teacher's voice so a bell, chime or special sound is helpful. The important thing is to get the rebels as busy and engaged as soon as possible. They can pass out supplies, run errands, and be in charge of the coats, for example. Kids who are power hungry need to be coached into leadership roles. They can take attendance, pass out papers, and write the quote of the day on the board. They want to have choices and control.

After an initial flutter of organization, get the class's attention, all eyes on you and tell them the goals for the day. I like to have the goals written as well as spoken, so that students who work more quickly or slowly than others can know what's coming next. It is also good to have an extra goal for the kids who work rather fast. Some students are busy bees, and feel like they have accomplished something when they complete a lot of work. They like to copy ten sentences to punctuate rather than three and think about what they are doing. As the teacher, you need a default lesson that is always available if some get done early.

In order to appear approachable and not too cold, the teacher needs a way to engage students in friendly banter. Talk about your favorite hob-by or pets. My Jack Russell was a forever safe way to reveal my own personality without giving out any personal information.

If you have a rowdy group, you can place that convex mirror I mentioned in the previous chapter near the

Focus on Students

Children on the autism spectrum – such as those who have Asperger's Syndrome – are usually uncomfortable with eye contact, but you can teach these kids to SLANT:

Stop,

Look,

Ask a question,

Nod, and

Track with your eyes.

If you talk to them by standing next to them, looking out at the room, it's easier for them to cope. They will accept a rule.

board so that you can see what the class is doing behind you while you write on the board. The less mature students need more authority rather than less. Offering too many choices tends to encourage pushing the boundaries of conduct.

There will be plenty of opportunity to set "norms" with a class. Norms are an agreed consensus about behaviors and are flexible and increase cooperation from the kids. Norms can be made regarding snacks, the bathroom pass, arrangement of chairs, ear-bud use and so on. Norms are not extended to school policies such as cell-phone use.

When you establish the rules for the year, it is helpful to keep them as "positive principles" rather than to try to label every possible negative behavior. Middle-schoolers, especially 7th graders, can look for any possible loophole in order to manipulate the situation. My last set of class rules follows, and I think it is a good set. This can be used as a student handout. You may want them to copy any rules they break in an after-school or lunch detention.

CLASSROOM RULES

1. **ANY behavior that interferes with learning is unacceptable.**

2. Be on time. Enter quietly, ready to work. Work silently on the starter until told to stop. We have an Enter door and an Exit door.

3. Be respectful to your teacher, other students and other staff at all times. This includes not only verbal communication (language), but also nonverbal communication (gestures) and attitudes. Clowning or distracting others is disrespectful, not only to the class, but also to yourself.

    - My desk is off limits. Do not help yourself to any items in my area. You may NOT use my chair. Listen to and follow directions without interruption. Questions when appropriate are fine.

    - No insulting, swearing, vulgar language or put-downs, not even in jest. No pushing, taking of personal items, or harming other people's materials.

    - Sloppy, quick work is unacceptable.

    - Any staff that comes to my room is my guest and should be treated as a guest.

4. Stay on Task. Stay on Topic. Do your best. Stay focused for the entire period. There are four kinds of class activities:

    - Silent work: Working independently; **no** talking

- Quiet Work: Working with partners; talking is required, volume must be appropriate for **private** conversation between partners
- Discussion/Reading aloud: Taking turns and listening to each person
- Activity: Learning through movement.
- Stay seated unless asked to put away materials, distribute materials, or do some other helpful task

CHAPTER 5

THE STOP EXERCISE

Within the first few days of class, I describe the Stop Exercise. This exercise is often called the "Listening Exercise" and is ancient, coming from the Vedanta philosophy that encourages people to begin and end all activities from stillness. Stillness, also understood as rest, is the move towards egolessness.

If you slow down your own voice and then gradually extend the "hold" part of the breath, the kids will slow down. After one minute say "good" which is the signal to open eyes and begin the next activity. You may check in with them by asking questions such as, "How was that?," "What was the effect of that?," "How do you feel?," or "What did you hear?"

Many kids will say "tired" or "hungry," which shows that they are actually getting in touch with the state of their bodies. If a kid says "happy" or "calm," you are heading in the right direction. Remind them that in many ways "feelings" are like weather. They are natural, they pass, and they change over the course of a day. There is no right way to feel. The whole spectrum of emotion is part of the human condition.

Focus on Students

Some kids will do almost **anything** to sabotage this exercise, basically to attract attention, gain power and relieve their own distress at being still. It's important to work with these students so they "buy into" the exercise at least enough so they are not disturbing other students.

As SoryuForall explained, "You must find the wisdom in what they are telling you... and work with that." If one of your students says, "I couldn't relax. I have thoughts in my head," do not intrude by asking, "What thoughts?" Instead, reply, "Great – you noticed your thoughts! Do you want to continue to notice your thoughts, or would you prefer to try something else?"

It's a good idea to keep your own eyes open and to tell the class that you are doing so. I've seen Cheetos fly, smirks, and all kind of silliness. Sometimes the kids think they look "dumb" if they sit still. You can ask a volunteer to sit still for a minute and ask the class if it looks awkward or stupid. It doesn't. If they insist that it "looks stupid," you might say that "self- control" is strong, not weak and to just try it for a time. Think about the attention of a cat watching a mouse hole or a dog watching a squirrel out of the window. Before bursting into action, they watch and listen intently. You might call this sitting the Hero Pose, or Sitting Strong, or, as the Mind Up program calls it, the "Core Practice." Sometimes I tell the kids that because they have the ability to reason, to be conscious and self–conscious, they must reflect the dignity and poise of being human. No other animal is SELF-conscious as is a human.

There will usually be one or two kids who resent and resist this exercise. Following are some helpful options. Ask each of these students what exercise they might like to try and then figure out how to support that.

- Have the student stand while he performs the Yoga Mountain Pose (super hero).

- Have the student try balancing on one foot.
- Have the student look out the window and gaze at some greenery.
- Have the student listen to the sound of his own breath.
- Have the student lead the exercise after some training.
- Offer to review the process with him during lunch.

Have the student repeat in his head a positive phrase such as "Every day in every way, I'm getting better and better." (Dale Carnegie was one of the original positive thinkers, and this phrase comes from his work.)

Those students who have Attention Deficit Disorder and/or Oppositional Defiant Disorder or who have been traumatized, will be reluctant to cooperate. You can only require that they *appear* to co-operate. When working with one good but challenging student, I reminded him, "It's only one minute. Tell yourself a story." The Stop Exercise will bring up resistance, as will many of the other practices described in this book. It is advisable that after a sincere effort on the student's part, if she/he is stuck, then take a rest, a moment to regroup. When doing this work, sometimes tears follow extreme levels of frustration. Protecting kids from any kind of loss of face in front of their peers is vital. No one, especially middle school boys, want to be embarrassed in front of their peers, and they will avoid any recurrence of an activity that might put their dignity in jeopardy.

This Stop Exercise will get old in about a week. At this point, it is helpful to add variety to the activity, such as standing, gazing at your hands, looking out the window, counting breaths, and so on. I used to instruct the students to "sit balanced and erect" during the Stop Exercise until my mentor pointed out that the seventh-grade boys were falling off their chairs laughing, so be careful that your language isn't promoting a connection that isn't conducive (ie: sex) to the exercise.

I found that using a Tibetan Singing Bowl was more riveting that just the voice. Students are eager to have the privilege of ringing it themselves, and there is a real technique to getting the bowl to hum. It can be rung three times and then students can listen until the sound fades into silence. Now if a bowl is not appropriate for your school, there are glass bowls and bar chimes that also resonate. The long fading sound that sustains the attention is what is important.

With some kids, the lure of the competition of listening and then raising their finger to indicate when they can no longer hear the sound works. It's important to stop any kind of mischief in the first few times so that the real power of the sound is observed.

Some ways to have it go better are:

- Have the script on CD or tape so you can move close to any mischief-maker or have a partner move around the room as you talk.
- Some variations for listening are:
    - Listen to sound tracks of various things and identify them.
    - Listen to the Peruvian flute music.
    - Listen to the special sound tracks created for meditation exercises.
    - Listen to the rain forest, birds or waterfalls sound tracks.
    - Listen to classical music, Gregorian chant or some kind of rhythmic African music.

THE STOP EXERCISE

Begin by saying, **"Let's come to a complete Stop,"** and then wait until all the students look at you. Read the following sample script or something similar of your own design:

"If you are comfortable with closing your eyes, good, allow your eyes to rest. If you prefer, you may look down at the table or your hands. Just sit up straight with your head held high. Feel balanced, still, and at ease. Feel the weight of your body in the chair, your feet on the floor, and the play of air on your face and hands.

"Now, remain quite still, and don't make any sounds. Let your listening expand to include all the sounds already in this room, all the sounds in the hall, and all the sounds in the building. Try to hear the tiniest, most delicate sound as far away as you can.

"Take a deep breath, filling up your diaphragm. It will feel like your stomach is rising. Hold until the count of three... 1, 2, and 3. Good. Release the breath. Again, hold until the count of three... 1, 2, and 3 slowly release.

Just rest in this wide-open attention for one minute.

CHAPTER 6

THE START EXERCISE

Focus on Students

Some students have difficulty remembering the instructions from school once they get home. The disconnect may be because there are no cues for the assignment, for example, notes on the board, posters and so on. When a student mentally reconstructs the environment of school, including the teacher's voice and face, they have a better chance to reboot the lesson.

Only a handful of students can organize themselves or have an intuitive sense of categories. The students who do not have an "inner urge" to keep their tools organized are often creative, energetic, articulate. It takes mental energy to sort things and place them into the logical folders or boxes. Kids who resist this think that it is a waste of time and they should be "doing their work" or "having fun" instead. The worst case of disorganization I ever saw was layers of papers of all subjects in one stack interspersed with leftover sandwiches, candy bar wrappers and broken pencils.

The START Exercise may be used every day or every other day. The student may need to be shown how to create the categories such as subjects: Math, Science, and English, etc. They will have to also develop Units. Sometimes it is safe to assume that if the papers are in chronological order, it's enough, but frequently papers need sets and subsets.

The teacher can laminate several copies of the START Exercise and post them on the wall. Have some for the students to take home, too, and put it on the school website. In fact if there is any procedure that you use frequently, you may want to create a protocol and have laminated copies of it handy for your classes. This allows students to do things like learning spelling words, editing papers, and expanding their sentences. It helps the teacher to save the energy that it would take to repeat the same process over and over.

The teacher can say, "Here is a way to get started on your work. You can copy it from our website and post it where you do your homework." Frequently, middle-school students are motivated by an emotional connection to the teacher. If they like the teacher or believe that the teacher likes them, they will work very hard in that class. A sense of loyalty develops which is why, during the START Exercise, students are asked to remember the faces of their teachers. Memory is supported by an emotional connection. Students in middle-school have a tendency to perform well for the teachers they like, and poorly for teachers they do not like.

You might notice that the START exercise is comprised of *action words*. That is a recommendation from experts who work with ADHD students who say that an Action is easier to understand than a vague description.

START	
SIT down	at your desk. Do the Stop Exercise for one minute.
Take out	all your papers and put them in the right categories
Agenda	check your Agenda Book.
Review	your day. Picture your teachers' faces: what did they ask you to do, the requirements? Write them down.
Time	*Look at the time. Write it down. Promise to concentrate on one task for 20-30 minutes.*

CHAPTER 7

ORGANIZATION

It is unlikely that a middle-school child will acknowledge the wisdom of your organization suggestions, but they do love games and "proof" that something will work. The Organizing the Deck Game was developed as a back door to prove to students that organization is indeed a "time and sweat saver." Its objective is to help students grasp the reasons for organization and to demonstrate categorizing.

I have used this game with several hundred students, and it has never failed to entertain and gain group participation. It was also passed along to other teachers who rewrote the directions I gave them and created the document below. Be aware that the child with a learning disability may be a little slower at "finding" the card, so you have to get a mean score of the time, that is, the most frequent time rather than an average which would be skewed by either very slow or very quick students.

ORGANIZING THE DECK

For this activity, you will need a deck of cards for each student, a time chart to keep track of times, and a stopwatch. Make sure that all the decks of cards are shuffled before you hand them out. To begin the activity, explain to the class that their task will be to find a specific card, the Target Card, when the cards are organized in different ways. Ask what some of the categories are that we might use to organize a deck of cards. Have them briefly discuss and predict what might happen.

When you finish this discussion, give the time chart and stopwatch to an assistant. Let that person know how the activity will proceed and describe what s/he will need to do. Next, instruct the students to put their decks of cards face down on the desks in front of them. Tell them to get ready to find the Target Card as quickly as possible. Also tell them that they should pull the card out of the deck and hold it up as soon as they find it. (Note that for Round One, the cards are unsorted, so the students don't need to sort their decks before the round starts. However, in each subsequent round, before the Target Card is selected, you will instruct the students to sort the cards in the way indicated below for each respective round.) Tell the assistant to pick the Target Card, hold it up, and say its name out loud.

As the students hold up their cards, the assistant uses the time chart to record the time it takes each student to find and hold up the Target Card in their own decks. When all the students have found their Target Cards, the assistant also records the average of the students' times. Repeat each round one more time, using a different Target Card for the two instances, so that you end up with two scores to average. (You may want to do the first round three times to make sure everyone gets the hang of it.) Tell the assistant to calculate the average of these two numbers. Finally, after each round, allow some time for observations. Here are some thought-provoking questions you might ask to guide the students' analyses:

- What do you notice about how fast you found the Target Card?
- How much time did you spend preparing for this round?
- Is there a trend or pattern?
- Do you think that too many categories might be problematic?
- Do you think that too few categories might be something to consider?
- The final round had the most subsets. Was it efficient or not?

When you've completed as many rounds as you decide to do, have the students discuss the purpose of sorting the cards into categories, the efficiency of different styles, and any other observations they made during the activity.

Round Descriptions:

Round One:	Whole deck (shuffled)
Round Two:	Red cards (shuffled), black cards (shuffled)
Round Three:	Face cards (shuffled), number cards (shuffled)
Round Four:	Suits (each suit shuffled by itself)
Round Five:	Suits (each suit in sequence)
Round Six:	13 sets of face cards and number cards

If time allows, do any other sets students think up. I ask them to organize their own card packs and then switch their seats, but not the packs, with someone else. You can add that if someone else can find an item in your system, then you have a system that is logical and well organized.

Finally, develop the students' discussion from the simple categorization of cards and toward the value of being organized in general. Ask them what benefits come from being organized. For example, this exercise demonstrates that you can locate things more easily and save time when you are organized. It also shows that the way you organize needs to work for you, not necessarily someone else. What is important is to have some sort of organizational system. Ask the students to think of examples of organizational systems that might help them, such as their agenda books or neatly sorted folders, accordion folders and binders.

CHAPTER 8

ALL ABOUT SOUND: SILENCE, TONE AND ATTENTION

Not every child is equally aware of his or her environment in the classroom. It is important that the kids can hear your directions clearly, talk softly enough to hear each other and not be distracted by buzzing, hums or clicks from any machines. Usually one or two students will be willing to be in charge of the Noise Level. You may want to draw on the board a visual aid like this:

Noise-o-meter

Goal	Current
1 or under	6

I ask the students what the effect of a really loud classroom is. Usually – the response is, "it gives me a headache," or "too distracting." Then I say, "If one is silent, how does a 10 level of noise sound like?" Invite them to make lots of talking noises, not screaming and tossing things around, just talking. Give a signal to stop. Then ask, "So what does 5 sound like?" Discuss that. Good. Then ask if someone would be willing to be the noise monitor for the day. Give them the white board marker, or whatever you use. As soon as the noise gets a little too much, look quizzically at the designated person. Get some kind of agreement with a nod or look on whether they should write a number.

Focus on Students

Some students on the autism spectrum or those who have sensory integration issues and cannot tune out distractions, are helped by plants, cork boards, room dividers or cloth bulletin boards which help cut the sound down.

Sometimes having their own choice in music on headphones works. If you do allow headphones, pre-select the music because making a choice can consume an enormous amount of time. Student may endlessly switch the music to reach finer and finer choice preferences.

I truly believe that working silently is the best option for creative, concentrated work, but not every culture or situation requires it or considers that it is a valuable asset. In the book called *Silence as Yoga*, Swami Paramananda says that in order to retain creative energy, it is useful to not blurt out every new idea you have and offer it up for discussion. In order to get in touch with your senses and allow the view to open up and penetrate deeper levels of awareness by touch, sound and sight, silence is needed.

Think about the times that you may have had a "spark" that made sense to you but was not fully formed. It is possible to drain that energy quickly by describing it to others, and it also opens up the door to discouragement and the doubts of others about your ability to execute the idea. It is better to work out the details yourself, committing to some form or words, and then, only when it is appropriate, get a review before you open it up to the public, should you need or request feedback.

It has been frequently observed in the education field that students practicing attention to detail can obtain a wealth of information through concentration. This single pointed attention is called *Ekagra.* This deeply focused attention when doing a task such as painting a wall or studying a text, reveals successive layers of information such as the viscosity of the paint requiring a specific brush, when one is using too much, when the paint will drip, if the second layer of paint should have a light touch, and so on.

Wide open, clear, relaxed attention, or *Prakaasha Citta*, is the basis for the Stop or Listening exercise. Focused, pointed attention and wide-open attention are considered two useful forms of attention. Two less useful forms of attention are "attention captured" which is *Moha* in Sanskrit, and "attention scattered" or divided, *kshipta* in Sanskrit.

When you have more languages to describe the functions of the mind, you'll have a way to present ideas to kids in terms that they will recognize as true. For example, I have noticed that any time my own attention is divided (*kshipta*), not present or not fully focused, there is stress and less efficiency. This stress may be barely noticeable, but it is cumulative, and, by the end of the day, it can take a toll on the nervous system.

The preference for silence doesn't mean that you don't ask for guidance if you are not certain about execution. That is different than blurting out every little thought you have. Some kids learn by giving themselves directions such as "I need to put my pages in here." Others like to ask questions as they work because it reinforces their learning. During collaborative activities, it is completely appropriate to talk about what they are observing. But quite often, students are not talking about the work but rather entertaining themselves with social chatter which is a waste of their time and energy.

Focused listening requires that our own minds be quiet so that we can truly hear what the other person is saying. This kind of silence requires controlling our own *Manas*, or head chatter. One of the hardest skills to develop is listening to others talk. Most of the time while pretending to listen, we are actually rehearsing what we want to say as a rebuttal. In contrast, real listening is both a revelation of the speaker and nourishing to both the listener and the speaker. An exercise that was tried during a long retreat I attended in Wallkill, New York, was called "Diction." We formed two lines of people in an open field. It was a splendid summer morning and there were birds, bees and cows in a nearby pasture.

Our text, in this case, Genesis from the King James Version of the *Bible*, was passed down each row. Our instructions were to say a stanza aloud. The listeners had to repeat the stanza from memory in exactly the same way as the original speaker. We were instructed to use the same pace, inflection, tone and so on. Then with each pass, we stepped about 3 or 4 feet away from each other to determine if we could still "hear" each other.

This exercise tests both attention and opens the participant to some surprising information. As we moved further away from each other, we could still hear quite clearly, but this was based on our attention to the speaker, not the distance the sound was travelling. If the focus was on the speech, the senses managed to receive it.

Next we learned that when a listener copies a speaker with the same inflection, pace, and tone, it shifts from outward manifestations to knowledge about the state of that being. Somehow, copying without personal interpretation, reveals the emotional state of the speaker. The degree of knowledge gained is proportional to how pure the interpretation is.

At the end of the exercise, we heard a cow from a nearby field *moo* really loudly, and it was evident that she wanted to participate too, but found to her dismay that she didn't have a human voice. We all laughed.

It may not be a good idea to tell anyone ahead of time what you think the exercise might reveal; instead keep memory and attention the focus of the practice. Don't be too surprised if other things are revealed.

THE HOARDER'S STASH

Have a student sit blind-folded on one side of the classroom or with her/his back towards the class. A set of valuables, like a ball, a toy, a book are placed near that student. These are that student's treasures.

The rest of the students try to sneak up and "steal" an object. If the blind-folded leader hears someone, s/he points directly at where that student is. The student that is discovered is "out" and joins the teacher as a silent witness. The exercise continues until all the students are out or all the items in the stash are stolen.

(This game was created by Soryoforall from Burlington, Vermont, USA.)

soryroforall @budsa.com

One listening exercise designed to sharpen listening skills is called **The Hoarder's Stash.** It is similar to a game you probably know, Red Light. To play Red Light, one person faces the wall while the rest of the players try to sneak up on him or her and touch the wall. The challenge is for the leader to turn quickly and catch the kids in action, and then they are out. The Hoarder's Stash exercise is similar to this in the sense that the group is trying to sneak up on the leader.

A "cloze" reading exercise of filling in the blanks of a well-known story can be done orally in order to teach collective focus on words. A part of the Parker school curriculum was to study political conflict and debate on both sides of a controversial issue. The topic that was chosen one year for the 7th and 8th graders was the Palestinian/Israeli conflict over land. The classes had reviewed the facts and politics from the Second World War and onward, but had not studied the fundamental premise that the Jews considered this land as their "promised land." The classes had not researched Biblical times when Moses led the Hebrew slaves out of Egypt into the desert. Luckily, many of the children did know the basics, but I set up the story as an "outloud" fill-in-the-blanks, and the students engaged in its retelling by answering as a group:

Once upon a time in Egypt, there was a man named ____________________. He was born to a Hebrew slave woman. Now the Pharaoh of the land of Egypt had been warned by a prophecy that a great leader would arise among the Jews and he was so afraid that he ordered that all the ____________________________ to be killed that year. The mother of _______________ was very smart so she put her baby in a _________________ and floated him down the ________________ where the palace was. The Princess and her Royal ladies were bathing in the river and they spotted the ____________.

The Pharaoh's daughter adopted the infant and raised him as her own child. When the boy grew up, a terrible thing happened. His brother, a cruel man, was beating a slave viciously, and Moses angrily ________________ him.

Now Moses was in big trouble but God told him that he had to go to the Pharaoh and tell him to ________________________. The Pharaoh said _______________________________.

So terrible plagues came to Egypt (continue).

My favorite student response to this practice was when Moses was telling the Pharaoh to "let my people go," he said, "in your dreams!" which was strangely appropriate.

Here are two more communication exercises: Mirror Listening and How Did Simon Say It.

The objective for the first activity is to have students observe the dynamics of communication. It contains elements of body language, emotional charge, word choice, tone, pace, inflection, and the speaker's perception.

Because this lesson can get rather noisy, you may want to send students into corners or the hallways to do it. Have the observers keep track of the time if you are out of range. Each complete set should be about 15 minutes. When the class has regrouped, have one member from each team share what they learned, heard or observed. Try to draw some conclusions or principles such as:

I keep on being put off by my own ideas.

It is important to ______, not change the words.

The tone of voice makes a difference.

I was distracted by the hall noise.

Write the student comments on the board.

An extension of this practice might be for the observer to ask the speaker a question or to coach the partners when a student is not explaining it well OR the repetition is not accurate, in order to clarify the intent, meaning and intensity. The next activities are about the TONE or inflection of language.

MIRROR LISTENING

Tell the class that they are going to doing a "Listening Mirrors "exercise where they will attempt to be a "mirror" or "video recording" to the student speaking. They are to listen without interrupting to the description from students who have been designated as speakers, and they need to observe and copy every detail of tone of voice, posture, and pace of words, word choice and emotional intensity.

Ask the class to think about an event that made them very sad, angry or frustrated. Let the group process and visualize that moment in time for a minute or two. Then divide the class into teams of three students each by counting ones, twos, threes. In the first round, the students counted as *ones* speak, *twos* listen, and the *threes* observe for accuracy. Then switch until each has had a turn in the different roles. The teacher calls "Time" for the switch.

Allow a little bit of extra time between each change for them to resettle.

You might say; ready, steady, go! before each turn.

Then give the speakers 2 minutes, timed, to tell their story, 2 minutes for the Listeners to repeat the story, and lastly have the observers give feedback on the accuracy of the repetition.

Because this lesson can get rather noisy you may want to send kids into corners, or the hallways to do it. Have the observers keep track of the time if you are out of range. Each complete set might be about 15 minutes- moving rather quickly. When the class has regrouped, have one member from each team – share out what they learned, heard or observed... Try to draw some conclusions or principles such as,

How Did Simon Say It

- Begin with a warm-up where you ask the class: Can the same sentence mean different things depending on HOW it is said? An example might be: So you want to come with us?

  The teacher says the sentence aloud and the students have to interpret the tone-emotional content. Write these emotions on the white board.

  So you want to come with us? An even tone that is sincere and welcoming (welcoming)

  So YOU want to come with us? Sorry kid, we are way too cool for you (patronizing)

  So you WANT to come with us? I'm getting aggravated with you and you are wasting time. You want to go or not? (impatient)

  So you want to come with US? That's a surprise. Either we are not your first choice or you are not our first choice (confused, vexed)

  So you WANT TO COME with us? Look this is a really dumb event, are you sure you have the time?

  Have students brainstorm different attitudes and emotions that are communicated by Tone. Write these on the white board and ask how is it is communicated.

  Have the student try different tones and emotions with a partner with the sentence:

  I'll give him that message

Another exercise for detecting tones that are offensive or hurtful, is the following:

Sarcasm is communicated by short statements, tossing the head, a raised eyebrow and a mock question. *So you think so?*

Describe: tone of intimidation, anxiety, impatience, sympathy, shyness, fear of the person you are speaking to, arrogance, bored, patronizing.

Break up into practice groups of 2 to 4 in each group. Give them sentences to try to manipulate the tone. Have the students write two originals.

1. *That's peachy.*
2. *Do you think that's true?*
3. *He doesn't even remember that he has a memory problem.*
4. *The whole point of our nervous system is to develop a sense of what is happening in the present and what is about to happen in the future.*
5. *The next frontier for exploration will be the sea bottom, not the skies.*
6. *This time, the wound is going to be slow to heal.*
7. *So where are all the teachers?*
8. *Not everyone from New Jersey acts like that.*
9. *That guitar riff was so cool.*
10. *I'm sorry, but did you say we were going to eat lunch at Friendly's*

Tell the students that when they return, they will say their best example of a definite tone, and the class has to guess what it is. Give them 10 to 15 minutes to practice.

When students return to their seats, use the Popcorn method (teacher calls first student, that student names the next student). Students shout out the "tone" together. If they disagree, discuss it. Put a check next to the tone word on the white board. Ask for a variety if one tone is over-used.

CHAPTER 9

THE PAUSE

As part of the program, I ask the students to "pause" at the end of each class after they have collected and packed their materials. (One of my students put his two hands up like a begging puppy and said "paws" which, along with being cute, grabbed the class's idea of fun.) Mindful practices teach us that there is a natural rest at the end of each activity and all activity has a cycle that begins, grows, peaks, completes and ends.

Sri Shantananda Saraswati the sitting guru of Northern India of the late 20th century, said that with the advent of electronics, we no longer have a natural rhythm to the day. With lights and electronics, we have made it possible to work or be entertained at any time of the day or night. Our mammalian nervous system is basically geared to wake up with the light, work during the day, slow down at dusk and then sleep when it is dark. For most of human history, if you were burning the "midnight oil," it was very poor light and had to be for an extraordinary occasion.

I wonder about the state of mind of people who, while walking through the grocery store, have the phone plugs stuck in their ear and are having a seemingly one-sided conversation in public as they pick out groceries. We presume that by adding a layer of frosting, music, or conversation that our life is enriched and pleasant. Is that really the truth of it, or are we adding layers of stress by trying to do multiple tasks at once? Is that really efficient?

The neuroscience on multi-tasking says that we are actually less efficient when trying to do two things at once. What usually happens when we switch back and forth from one task to the other very rapidly, is that there is a "hesitation" after the switch. Listening to music on headphones is an example of this. A kind of double bind occurs when we reject the simplicity of taking a walk in the woods and hearing the crunch of gravel beneath our feet and birds singing, in preference to listening to music on headphones. We are ignoring reality and becoming disconnected from the world.

Recently in the Northeast, we had the good fortune of having a snow storm that knocked out power for several days. The refrigerator stopped humming, I couldn't play with the computer, life slowed down enormously, we cleaned, cooked, bathed, talked, hauled wood, lit candles. Cooking by candle light was a real delight. I noticed I was placing items where they were "supposed" to be and being careful about the doors and such. While preparing for the evening, I had dropped bits of candle wax on the floor, so I was hunting in a nearly dark basement for the right kind of scraper. Intuitively, my hand went out into the box, and I found exactly what I was looking for. The darkness of the room required memory, sensitivity and another kind of "light." All that slowing down and simplicity highlighted how "noisy" our lives are. Even if we don't realize that we are "jacked up" by the TV news and the constant flow of information, it affects us.

With all this ever-increasing pace of life, nearly limitless distractions on the Internet and young people's social lives, there is no recognizable break in the onward rush towards the end of the day. The push to do more and more actually takes a toll on the nervous system. In schools, for example, there are often no breaks between classes which makes it hard for the student to retain his/her learning because they don't consolidate that first impression of a lesson. Therefore, the antidote to this onslaught of rushing and stimulation for them is REST or Pause for a short while.

When describing this cycle I put this on the board:

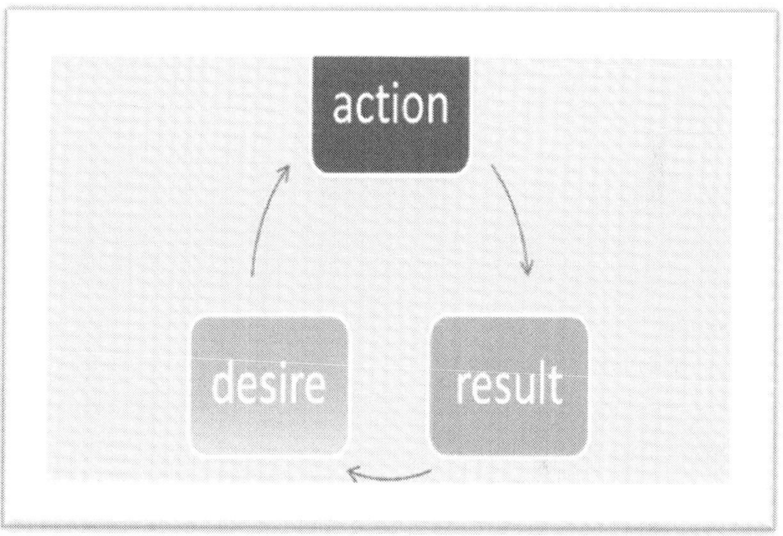

Next I ask students to talk about how it feels to be on the "Go" all the time. You can write down their comments. At this point, you might try asking the students how it feels to put their head down on the pillow when they are happily tired. They can close their eyes and just remember that moment of snuggling down into the blankets and the coolness of the pillow. Next you might ask how it feels to do that. Ask, "What would be the benefit if you could do that from time to time during the day?" Then I add the last step as in the diagram below:

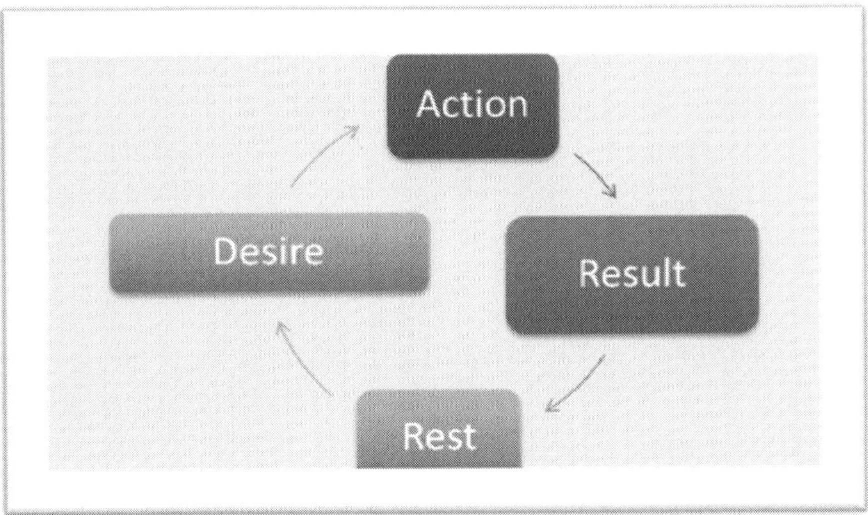

Students may agree to try this experiment – The Pause – or you can just ask for it. For example, in order to interrupt that frazzled feeling, ask students to put away their materials; then "Pause" before the class ends. The "Pause" at the end of class allows the nervous system to calm down so any residual tension is not carried forward. An additional benefit of a period of rest and reflection after intense learning strengthens the learning. Try the following:

THE PAUSE

Instruct the students to put away all their materials and then stand behind their chairs.

Then say, "Stand tall and strong. Feel your feet on the floor. Become aware of yourself and the room. Consider what you have just completed. Rest. After about 30 seconds to one minute you say "good. Dismissed"

My students love to invent different variations of The Pause, such as:

- The Gangster Pause, which means looking "tough"
- The Tree Pose Pause, referring to the Tree Pose position in Yoga
- The Can-You-Actually-Hear-a-Pin-Drop Pause
- The Say-a-One-Word-Impression-of-the-Previous-Work Pause
- Breathe deeply
- Stare at a focal point
- Listen to the sound of the water fountain or buzz from machines in the room
- Freeze-In-Whatever-Position-You-Are-In Pause

The Vedic reason for this Pause is to acknowledge that the results of all actions is returned to the Absolute. When a person releases his "claim' on the work, it allows the ego a moment to let go of whatever results have come from the work that was just completed. The objective is to be the instrument for the energy to meet the needs of creation. If a sense of shame or pride ties us to the result, more attachment is created. It is the same sentiment as the Christian aphorism, "Lord, let me be an instrument for your use."

Your school will have its own culture and emblems so you may end up with the Silent Panther Pause or the Bear-Waiting-To-Swipe-a-Fish Pause. Remember that the younger, rambunctious children will not tolerate being still unless it seems fun. This exercise is ideal for these students.

CHAPTER 10

THE GUNAS

According to Vedanta, the *gunas* are the great states of energy or levels of vibration that permeate all of material creation. Just as water is liquid, solid and gas, the *guna* indicates how dense material is. Since the Eastern tradition views all of creation, whether material or spiritual, as a continuum of the same substance, it also points to how awake or conscious a thing or being is. Some physicists describe matter as being a swirl of particles, waves, vibrations or molecular patterns; this is aligned with that view. People can think of it as a spectrum of the most concrete to the most subtle or perhaps the least alive to the most alive. In Advaita, the assumption is that that which is eternal, immutable and infinite is REAL and alive, while the ephemeral, finite, and material world is "not real." This is the opposite of our usual perception. This view presumes that our world as we perceive it is Illusion or *Maya*. There is a Sanskrit aphorism that states, "Everything exists in Name and Form only." That is, all objects are in some form of growth or decay but are essentially the same substance, *consciousness,* which, in its current state, is named this or that form. Since the universe is in constant flux, creation, or *Purusha* as it is called in Sanskrit, manifests in ways that are governed by the *guna* and humans are subject to its influence.

Focus on Students:

If a child has an abusive or chaotic home life, gentle reminders to behave often don't work. Some students are so used to extreme amounts of anger that the teacher might not be taken seriously if the same amount of "force" isn't being used. Take the child aside and negotiate a signal for them that means "Stop it right now." Follow through always. It appears to take five times the energy to correct rotten behavior as it does to initiate it.

The Sanskrit names for the *guna* are: *Satva, Rajas* and *Tamas.*

Satva is considered pure, generous, balanced, attentive, awake, but still.

Rajas is passionate, restless, full of desire, acquisitive.

Tamas is dull, sleepy, oblivious, crystallized.

The rise and fall of civilizations, organizations, the seasons, organic life, and individuals can all be seen in stages of birth, growth and decay. There are positive and negative aspects to each of these levels. For example, winter in the North is considered *tamasic* because it is cold, still, asleep, but, at the same time, this rest is also a natural part of the cycle. Spring can be considered *Rajasic* because of the fluidity and all the flowers popping up and animals creating. A summer sunrise might be considered *Satvika* because of the sense of still alertness, quiet potentiality. In relation to human consciousness, this describes how awake one is and how sensitively connected to others or aware.

There is an intuitive or self-evident logic to describing states of energy in this way. It is fun for students to discuss which *guna* best describes how, for example, foods make you feel or times of the day. It seems to be easily recognizable that pizza is heavy and *tamasic* and fruit is *Satvika*. Although the concept is easily understood, it was also useful to describe the *gunas* to the kids as **Sloth energy, Tiger Energy** and **Swan energy** and avoid the Sanskrit terms which might cause controversy. (Using Sanskrit words might be interpreted as teaching religion, not allowed in most schools.)

After a discussion with seventh graders about the states of energy being sleepy, dull, active-passionate, awake and calm, I have asked students which animal they thought could represent a certain *gunas*, and they usually guessed these animals right away. I brought in pictures of a sloth, swan and tiger. It delighted me that students usually agreed. The symbolism for this can vary; it is important only that the concept be portrayed accurately. For high school students who are more sophisticated in their understanding, you may be able to find psychologically based words such as: *Oblivious, Active*, and *Awake* which will stimulate their thinking.

My students noted that swans can be big, nasty birds, but they also look gorgeous floating on the water; although they appear still, there is a lot of power underneath. So the Swan became the symbol of *Satva*. There are also references in Hindu mythology about the Absolute being symbolized as a swan. A tiger with its restless pacing, subtle aggressiveness and power, captures the essence of *Rajas*. You might even extend the metaphor that the tiger is also moody, unpredictable, and alternately lazy or intense while tracking its prey. The attachment to hunting its victim might be used to relate to the concept of attachment to a goal. The image of a sloth languidly hanging from a tree with its long limbs and droopy shape certainly embodies the I image of indolence, turpitude and sleepiness.

The purpose of identifying the different *gunas* is to help the students to be aware of their own physical and mental states plus that of the surrounding environment. After students get a handle on these concepts, they often begin to understand the possibility of adjusting something to compensate. For example, if everyone is getting sluggish and inattentive, then opening a window, a bit of a stretch or the breath of fire might be just the thing to increase the energy level. It is important to note that although *Satva* may seem desirable, there is nothing inherently bad about any *guna*. *Gunas* just happen. All of our physical, mental and emotional systems are suffused with them. It is also believed that one can't simply jump from *Tamas* to *Satva,* but rather needs to get more energized in order to become awake.

The chart on the next page is an attempt to illustrate the three *gunas* and the three levels within each *guna* that are referenced in Vedanta philosophy. A quote is included that implies the general attitude and behavior within the level. The theme of the chart is that the lower the *guna* level, the more self-absorbed and isolated; the higher the *guna* level, the more aware of others and the environment, more generous and flexible in attitude. *Gunas* which suffuse the mind and body are constantly in flux and can be pushed in one direction or another.

SATVA	**Swan** Artful service	Joy, knowledge, freedom, appreciation, gratitude, blending ideas skillfully, accepting set-back calmly, understanding needs of others. Generous, saying little but powerfully, confident but quiet, can lead but does not show off. Aha moments of deep insight
	Elephant *The joy of participating*	Enthusiasm, contentment, waits for turn, prepared and thoughtful, plans ahead, synthesizes information, enjoys others' views, polishes off work. Good critical thinking
	Seal *This is my lucky day*	Hopeful, optimistic, cooperative, efficient and considerate, helps others, responds to need, may be disappointed when bliss ends. Understands the difference between what is good and what is popular
RAJAS	**Tiger** *Let's get it done*	Passionate, creative, cheerful but will sulk if corrected, cooperative, joins groups. Dislikes delays, may leave unfinished project or lack persistence
	Squirrel *We do it this way*	Conflicting desire, impatience, attached to personal system. Self-aggrandizement, busy, seeks praise and attention, productive but wastes time or too chatty. Can't predict reaction or consequences of actions
	Parrot *As Cool as you*	Gets angry if interrupted, opinionated, passionate, resentful if thwarted, tries to be Cool. Easily overwhelmed, wants easy and immediate pay-off. Doubt but energy, Insecurity but has goals, active but careless, attached to own ideas, stubborn, wants only fun
TAMAS	**Penguin** *As long as I belong*	Wants to belong, complains about others, follows the leader, thinks that popular means good, mean- spirited, will make small attempts, unoriginal, does the minimum to get by
	Walrus *Don't bother*	Shame or pride, unworthiness or gloating, jealousy, anger, crabby, selfish, resentful-hostile, blames others, distorts reality, making it harsher than is true, negative framing
	Sloth *Nobody cares about me*	Sluggish, dull, refuses to try, hopeless, depressed, unable to accept that effort would improve situation, unable to see solutions

"A rarefied form of the *gunas* is the substance of the psychological organs – *manas, buddhi, ahamkara, citta* – the mind, the intellect, the ego and the subconscious. A gross form of the same *gunas* appears as the five elements – earth, water, fire, air and ether. Therefore, there is a fraternity of feeling between the mind inside and the object outside, since both of these are constituted of the same *gunas*, as it has already been referenced in a statement of the Bhagavadgita: guṇā guṇeṣu vartante" (B.G. III.28). (http://swamikrishnananda.org/patanjali/raja_29.html)

These *gunas* are remarkable forces that cannot be controlled by ordinary effort. They are remarkable because they are our masters. We are made up entirely of them, and we are subjected to them in every way. Every fiber of our being is nothing but the *gunas*. This is actually the difficulty of self-mastery. The mastery over the *gunas* is mastery over one's own self.

For example, a compliment to a child can raise her spirits and energy levels, while a shaming or toxic comment to a child who is being turbulently active can force her into being quiet, but it can lower her ability to connect with the activity. It would be wiser to suggest that she focus on the work or consider how the turbulent behavior distracts others.

CHAPTER 11

GRADING

Much of my work has been with students who have difficulty with consistent effort. Whether it was a chaotic home life, uneven mental energy, learning disabilities or whatever, these young people had good days and bad days, the latter usually outnumbering the former. With a traditional grading system, these students will typically get something like: 65, 38, 92, 70, and 0, which averages to a 53%. They often, therefore, fail which seems to defeat the point of coming to school, especially when one or two failing grades for the term means failure. This didn't make sense for students with motivation problems so I created a system where every piece of work they did was a "plus." For every correct answer, every paper done, every positive move, the student earned credit towards a good grade.

The days in the term were counted, minus a few days for typical absences, field trips and other interruptions. For each day, students could earn credit: about 45 minutes worth of work was equal to 20 points (the highest), with fewer points for easier work and more for harder work. Usually, each correct answer counted toward the overall points for the day. A typical week was worth 100 points, and I would give extra credit for pro-social behavior such as organizing and good attitudes. The terms were usually 12 weeks, which meant 1200 points was an A plus. This system makes every bit of work done count as a positive. Points cannot be lost after they have been earned.

This system made sense for most kids. They felt like they got paid for what they did well and not penalized for what they messed up. I knew I had succeeded when I overheard one student telling another who was new to my class, "Don't worry, just do your work. It will be fine."

Praise, reinforcing the positive, creating a sense of unity rather than competition are essentials for a happy class. They reduce stress because the focus is on what is "correct" rather than error. The Vedic principal is the one of letting go of past errors and starting fresh each and every day. There are already enough events that cause these children stress, so why add shame?

If someone wants to check her grade, put the number of points plus (00) and then divide by 1200. That is the exact percentage of work out of 1200 that she has earned in points.

The following table provides correspondences between the number of points earned, percentage earned, and letter grades:

Points	Letter Grade	Percentile
1200	A+	97 percent
1150-1200	A	94
1101-1149	A-	91
1050-1100	B+	87
1001-1049	B	84
950-1000	B-	81
901-949	C+	78
850-900	C	75
801-849	C-	72
750-800	D+	69
701-749	D	66
650-700	D-	63
601-649	F	60
650 points out of a possible 1200 is "just" passing. That is the equivalent of doing a tiny bit more than 50% of the work.		

One caveat is that a typical cycle for some of these kids is to "coast" until two or three weeks before the end of the term and then to hurry up and do reams of sloppy, quick work. You can anticipate that they will work harder and faster toward the end of the term, so try not to make the work too easy at the beginning of the term.

I also wanted the kids to feel "in charge" of their own grades, so I asked them to keep track of the points they were earning. The following table is a smaller reproduction of the handout I gave them, which was a full 8 x 11 sheet to facilitate easier record keeping.

									1200
									1100
									1000
									900
									800
									700
									600
									500
									400
									300
									200
10	**20**	**30**	**40**	**50**	**60**	**70**	**80**	**90**	**100**

Each student was given a folder in which to staple the chart and another page to write down the assignments. As they got points for each assignment, they colored in the chart according to the number of points earned. On the assignment sheet, they noted the date, the assignment and the points earned. I also had a master copy of all the assignments given that they could refer to. Students were asked to keep the correct papers in that folder or binder until the end of the term. This was the "proof" so there were no arguments.

A learning disability, no matter what kind, requires more energy and more vigilance from the child in order to compensate for the tendency to make errors. It is very hard to be in a mind/body that does not operate efficiently. Furthermore, learning disabilities are like a blind spot to a driver in a car; the student is unaware that there is an error until another set of eyes reviews it. Imagine how disappointed you would be if your best effort resulted in glitches that you were unaware of making. Extra time, extra support and extra effort on the child's part are required to succeed. So if you see an exhausted kid or days when the child is less efficient than is typical, it shouldn't surprise you.

If you are required to write some sort of narrative in your progress reports, you want to pass out index cards to the students and ask them to answer the following questions.

Name *three* things you enjoyed doing this term

Name *two* things you found challenging

Name *one* thing you found helpful.

If you see 125 students a day, you can't possibly get to know them all so this little device will make you look like a "super teacher."

Another different, but equally good, way to grade students is the 'portfolio method' that is used, as in many others, by the charter schools known as the Coalition of Essential Schools. This method has caught on in the last few years as a creative and viable alternative to the classic methods of evaluation. After each grade or division establishes standards for achievement, the teachers grade the students as: Just Beginning, Approaches, Meets or Exceeds Standards. The students must revise his/her work until a certain number of projects "meet" the standard for that grade. What is built into this system is "mastery" of a particular skill. Some students find it easier to master "artistic expression" rather than a "text analysis." Nevertheless, a range of skills is required. Then the students present their work to parents and friends in a celebratory exhibition called a "GATEWAY."

The common sense of this system is evident because, instead of studying a topic for a time, taking a test and then never returning to the topic even if a student has failed to learn the material, requires a child to revise until mastery is achieved. This presents proof that the target skill is evident in their work.

I knew this made sense to kids when one older child explained to another, "it's like getting paid when you finish the job. If you don't finish, you can't collect your paycheck." The teachers are then utilized as "coaches" to help the students get their work done. The responsibility for learning is placed on the student. In November of their first year, some of 7th graders at the Parker would see their "gateway" as a far distant goal, and they felt entitled to coast, take their time and so on. But after the first round of "Gateways" in January, most students realized that revising and meeting all of the requirements of the school required that they work hard and consistently most of the time.

Focus on Students

A great strategy for "planning" a project is planning backwards. Set the date when an assignment is due, count back to a time when the student should have a rough draft, back again for research notes completed and back to resources located. Allow some time for unexpected delays. This prepares the students to pace themselves and not wait (which is common) until the last possible second. Older students could visit the classroom and make this recommendation to the newer students who might then consider it more seriously from them than from a teacher.

CHAPTER 12

PERSONAL LEARNING PLANS

At the Parker school setting goals, outlining the steps to get to them and then reflecting on whether or not you have achieved those goals was a big part of the program. An important point to keep in mind is that the adolescent brain can set goals, but frequently loses track of the sub-steps to reach those goals. Another highly relevant factor is that this cannot be a parental goal or the teacher's goal; it has to be something that is truly of interest to the child. For example, a teacher may also find that student goals such as becoming a NBA basketball player or a rock star are highly unrealistic, but instead of trying to discourage such lofty, far-reaching goals, focus on the sub-steps that would logically prepare the student for that goal. In the process, the student will be gaining skills and exploring options.

Think about how you perceive directions to go to a certain destination. In your mind, you picture the destination, then you may fill in the turns or landmarks for the first few miles, next the middle markers, and finally the arrival.

Adolescents do not have a well-developed capacity to picture and sequence the directions. It is just too much information at once. So anything you can do to break down the steps, put them in order and present an example of the finished project will help students plan, revise, sequence and set their goals.

The primary reason to set a goal is the fulfillment and happiness at mastering a skill or accomplishing something previously unattained. Time spent on discussing goals and how to track progress is never a waste of time. They need to be specific, measurable and have delineated sub-steps.

GOALS EXERCISE

Ask the student to think about their strengths and weaknesses and list them.

Take one of the strengths and imagine accomplishing some kind of wonderful skill mastered with that strength. Fill in the details of being congratulated and celebrated. Visualize this. Draw a picture or talk about the feelings it engenders.

Next, reflect on 3 things the student can do to reach that goal. Figure out a time-line of how often a skill needs practice or benchmarks. List these steps.

How will they know when they have reached the goal? Have them describe how they will know. The goal has to measurable, and there has to be evidence. This achievement has to be student-centered, not because the teacher said so. After they have completed the template with a strength, repeat the process with a challenge of weakness.

CHAPTER 13

ELECTRONIC ENTERTAINMENT AND SOCIAL ENGAGEMENT

As I have discussed before, our mammalian nervous system is geared to wake up with the light, work during the day, slow down at dusk, and then sleep when it's dark. As recent as fifty years ago, people were not "wired" into an electronic stream of information, as well as exposed to continual electric light and the buzzing of machines. We now have a choice to walk around with phones or music in our ears and have access to electronic games anywhere and anytime. This assault on the senses includes neon signs, billboards, radios in cars, and so on. A stream of news, mostly negative and fear-based, and advertisements that use the most sophisticated methods grab our attention constantly. When I was a child, the Sabbath and Sunday were days to slow-down and re-create yourself; now even that rest is often ignored or gone.

While watching television in a kind of feverish delirium during a recent illness, I noted that everything on television is designed to grab our attention and sell us stuff. It's all devised to create desire, so to speak, to buy, get, achieve, and so on. The implication is that buying, getting, achieving, and similar activities will create happiness, a false assumption which has been widely studied. One of ironies of this intrusiveness is that we often subconsciously resist paying real attention because it feels manipulative. We know that we should not totally accept the sales pitch. Nevertheless, current Internet marketing techniques use analyses of our interests, web searches, and mouse clicks to formulate their promotions and advertisements; we do not have complete control of our reality.

So, along with television and its effects, we also are faced with the all-pervasive Internet. The current generation, sometimes called the "Internet Generation" or "Generation Z" (following "Generation X" and "Generation Y"), are people born from the mid-1990s on. In the western world, most of this generation has never experienced life without the world wide web, which was increasingly available after 1991. They often began playing video games and visiting social networking websites as soon as they could hold a remote or use a computer. What effect does this have on their lives? One of the most noticeable results is that they often don't sleep as much as they should because they are engaged in social media or electronic games. At an age when their bodies require increased rest in order to grow new cells, their circadian rhythm resets to feeling tired at 11 pm or midnight and subsequently wants to wake up at 11 am the next day. Kids have frequently told me that they played a video game until 2 am, in part because it was available in their rooms. Often, when doing homework, kids are simultaneously chatting, gaming, etc. Although our students do play "Strategy" games, which range from traditional games like chess to modern games, they more often play "Action" or "Adventure" games, many of which are aptly-named "Shooters." These are essentially target practices where the only change is how fast you can "shoot" a weapon while cruising through a nightmarish, post-apocalyptic landscape where the mutants are out to get you. These nightmarish images presumably work their way into the psyche, and I am sure many dreams, not to mention, nascent addictions which reflect their influence.

Research has shown that the power of video games over boys seems to be particularity insidious. Boys play an average of 13 hours a week versus girls who play 5 hours per week. Boys are more likely to become addicted to video games and have poor grades because of the time spent "using" rather than doing homework. Hitting a moving "evil" target isn't as much of a cognitive challenge as, for example, writing an assigned essay. (Frontline: *Inside the Teenage Brain*, January 31, 2002, PBS)

Furthermore, "adolescents who play more than one hour of console or Internet video games may have more intense symptoms of ADHD or inattention than those who do not. Given the possible negative effects these conditions may have on scholastic performance, the added consequences of more time spent on video games may also place these individuals at increased risk for problems in school." (Ko, Chen, et al)

A challenging convergence of budding sexuality, poor consequential thinking and a desire to belong often occurs in the early teen years. Just when the need to be seen as attractive and sexy emerges, an inability to predict long term consequences is also in place. Young girls put themselves at risk with evocative poses and images on the internet that can float around forever. Boys, more often, will create more reckless portraits having to do with violence and superhuman strength to boost their reputations. Thoughtful Dads (if there are any at home; if not, other male adults) should move into the boys' turfs because the rather primitive idea that muscle makes the rules can put Moms at a disadvantage. The FBI and USA.gov document the most extensive problems with internet safety, so if there are serious concerns, parents can search there.

Another factor to consider is that these games generally, but not always, feed the desire for aggression and power, so the heroic model can be violent and crude. Kids crave heroes and want to emulate their talents and skills. The video game kind of hero is usually antisocial. The values that students are being taught by this kind of hero do not support what we need to thrive as a society, specifically, co-operation, mutual respect, integrity, critical thinking and restraint, in other words social emotional intelligence.

Students of this generation do not always have a clear idea of what a hero is. I recall a rather confused young man who thought that one radio commentator was a hero because he swore on the radio; the student thought this was great. You may want to discuss that a hero is not necessarily popular or cool.

So what can you do as a teacher? First, you can offer models of real heroism by reading stories of people who contribute to society. *The Chicken Soup for the Soul* series (edited by Jack Canfield/ www.jackcanfield.com) gives many examples of ordinary people who step outside of their comfort zones and set examples of unselfishness, love, sacrifice or standing up to a negative force. Some of the more famous heroes, Gandhi, Nelson Mandela, Abraham Lincoln, Mother Theresa, Clara Barton are widely available as resources, and Robert Bennett's *The Book of_Virtues* is a good source for wisdom and heroism.

In the beginning of the year, many teachers send home a letter introducing themselves to parents. That letter often includes expectations for the class, the amount of homework and other recommendations. In relationship to the information we now have about the Internet, you can include the following advice in your letter:

1. Have video game and internet time be limited to the weekends and not as soon as homework is done. This curtails the desire to be quick and sloppy just to get it done.

2. That a study area be created where the student can work with few distractions.
3. That parents consider monitoring their children's use of the internet during homework time and getting software that will track them.

The internet is changing all the time which requires that parents get involved in providing guidelines and rules before their children become too adventurous. The current software that protects computers from viruses, hacks and malicious tracking also has safety options for supervising children. This software sets limits on what they can watch on YouTube or other websites they can visit. It also will notify a parent if an attempt has been made to break the rules; some of them even record chats. It will also verify, if asked, pictures and how your child is portraying him/herself online.

Even mature kids, if given an opportunity to seek forbidden fruit, will do so at certain stages of development. Parents need to discuss their concerns with kids, agree to guidelines and follow through with supervision. I will admit that, when forbidden to use a certain game for more than 60 minutes a day, my son would get himself up at 5 am to play it. So nothing is foolproof.

For your students, you can present articles that help them understand how much sleep they need and why. You might also open up a discussion of the relative long-term value of video games versus sports, playing music, doing homework, and so forth. The kids will probably win this one, but you can at least help them understand the consequences of their choices and what their brains actually need.

II

COGNITIVE YOGA PRACTICES

CHAPTER 14

REST

Chapter 14 through 29 are practices that can be scattered throughout the year.

Children love variety, and it's important that different practices are offered to suit different learning styles and interests. Following is a restful activity, The Gold Coin, for the group, if you are in the mood. The image is supposed to help the kids relax and follow a direction for a brief period. After a "Stop" of about minute:

THE GOLD COIN

Imagine the most beautiful beach that you can. It has soft yellow-white sand; the water is turquoise, and nearly translucent at the shore. Gentle winds are blowing. Imagine that you would like to go for a swim and you walk slowly into the water. As you get in deeper, you find that you can see everything in a shimmering light under the water and, magically, you can breathe too. You sit down in the deep water and while looking up, a gold coin appears on the surface. It glitters in the sunlight and then drifts down, slowly swinging and flipping as you quietly watch it. Then you reach out, open your hand and let the coin land on your palm. You are flooded with joy and peace. Next, you rise to the surface and swim ashore. Now quietly return to room awareness.

Another kind of Rest is provided by an image of all of the world's activities as going on inside of you. This provides a sense of the observing witness while activities are a part of the cycle of life that emerges and passes. This is a reverse of feeling small and overwhelmed. It taps into an impression of vastness that minimizes everyday upsets. It is important to pause after each line in order to allow the description to fully take hold in the child's mind.

THE GIANT BALLOON

Visualize an energy field around your head like a halo. Now expand this field to include your whole body and outwards. While breathing deeply, let yourself expand this "balloon self" to include everyone and everything in this room. Let your listening extend and become aware of the entire building and the land around it. Now gently expand again, including the town and the surrounding towns. Think about all the things that people do, the hospitals, the cars on the road, the animals in the woods, the restaurants, the businesses. Now enlarge your view and include the entire state, the rivers, the mountains, the big cities, the ribbons of highways. Expand again to include your entire area of this country. Become aware of the entire section of the country as if you were in a space ship. Now, going even further, become aware of all the countries, the vast oceans, the polar ice caps, the different kinds of cultures. Inflate and spread out this light to include the entire solar system and the universes beyond. After a time, the teacher says, "Good. Slowly bring yourself back to room awareness as I count down from 10 to 1."

Technically speaking, the following script is hypnosis. This idea, originating from Ormond McGill, was presented to a class in California for the International Hypnosis Foundation. Ethically, the Vedic tradition holds that it is wrong to interfere with anyone's free will, so hypnosis that imposes an idea isn't acceptable. However, asking permission to guide someone to a relaxed state can be very welcomed.

The teacher says, "I am going to give you a piece of hard candy, but don't put in your mouth until I say to." When everyone is ready say, "OK, put the candy on your tongue and let it rest there. As the candy melts in your mouth, with each sweet taste, you will feel more and more at rest. As I count down from 10, you will go deeper and deeper into stillness and calm. You taste the candy; it brings you a sense of peace and safety."

1. You are allowing your body to relax and let go.
2. Your eyelids are so heavy, your body is comfortable and at ease.
3. Your breath comes and goes easily, nothing bothers or distracts you.
4. You are going deeper and deeper into profound relaxation.
5. As the sweetness rises in your mouth, a sense of protection and love envelops you.
6. You are more still now, going deeper and deeper into your deepest level of awareness
7. You are calm and centered and at ease with yourself and the universe.
8. You are very, very still.
9. While breathing deeply , you are refreshing your mind and body
10. You are profoundly tranquil and at ease.

After a time of snoozing or relaxing, the teacher says, "Alright, we are going to return to room awareness and the present moment, feeling refreshed and alert. As I count up from 1 to 10 you will gradually awaken." Then the teacher says:

1.) I am gradually returning to awareness
2.) I am feeling positive and happy
3.) It is time to be alert
4.) I am happy to be here now
5.) ....continue your own invention until 10

There are several practices that evolve around the principle of the Third Eye, and the development of intuition with its use. To give the little ones a focal point, you might do the following after The Stop.

Take the tip of your finger and touch your tongue. Now place that drop of water in the middle of your forehead just above your eyes.

Sitting up tall and strong, feel that place on the skin of your forehead. Let your eyes gently close. While they are closed, look at the spot on your forehead.

Imagine that tiny spot as a great blue ocean.

The waves are going into your own mind. You become fascinated by the beautiful rush of water and gentle movement of the waves. Breathe deeply, synchronizing with the waves. After some time, let your eyes return to normal position. Slowly open them. Open and close them three times. Then return to looking out and room awareness.

"Oppositional" kids are kids "at war" with authority figures. They resist and resent most directions unless they have a special attraction for them personally. I suspect that if a child feels betrayed by the adults in her life, she likewise feels that she can behave in irresponsible and hostile ways. The chances are very high that "stopping" or quiet introspection will make these kids uncomfortable because it can present a chance that emergent trauma memories will bring up toxic shame. Constant activity is also a way to keep depression away. Besides it's fun to be disruptive. It feels powerful because all eyes are on the student for having the nerve to battle with an adult. These children are frequently cruel, and their degree of self- centeredness and lack of empathy for others hovers in the area of narcissism.

I have seen many student try to evade, avoid, or destroy these peaceful exercises, often claiming that they don't work, or they're a waste of time. This happens when it looks like "not everyone" is on board or the school doesn't support Mindfulness, or you might have a negative leader.

Here are some ideas: You can ask them to hold a Yoga pose, you can offer an enriching text of some kind to read quietly or challenge them to form a safe-house picture in their mind and meditate on that.

I honestly don't always know how to deal with hostile kids who have the no-rules-for-me attitude, especially if the administrators do not give support. Those kids have to be removed if they disturb other students or some kind of compromise has to be reached. The handful of kids I met who were truly oppositional could not be depended on to keep up their end of a deal or a bargain. They would agree to do something and then fail to follow through. They did not feel bound to reciprocate kindness. The only thing that appeared to work – although not consistently – was to give attention to them by connecting to an activity that they truly enjoyed.

CHAPTER 15

ENHANCING THE EMOTIONAL IMPACT OF THE TEXT

Reading comprehension requires that the student empathize with the character in the story. After a student can read and comprehend the words, interpretation and real meaning require an emotional connection to the text. This chapter offers three exercises, each of which promotes the requisite empathy for real, fundamental understanding of the subject matter. Although all three achieve the same objective, they are considerably different, thereby satisfying the needs of a variety of diverse classroom environments.

This first exercise comes from the Parker School where the students usually had a great time creating the scene:

> Have the student pick a section from a text, discuss the body positions and facial expressions of the characters and then create a "tableau" that recreates the dramatic moment in that story. The scene hopefully has two or three characters that can be caught in a "stop action" type of pose. Students are evaluated on how well they translate the text into a scene, and they are asked to reflect in writing what they were trying to achieve and what their strategies were.

When I was working at Parker, one teacher asked if we could somehow simulate the emotional state of the character in a story. At the time we were reading the book, *Somehow Tenderness Survives: Stories of Southern Africa* by Hazel Rochman (Harpers/Teen, 1990). In one of the stories, the narrator, a little African boy, describes the night that the South African police broke into his family's shack looking for his parents. In order to heighten the emotional impact of the story, we created the protocol below:

> After reading the text as a class, prepare for the exercise by telling one group of students to form a circle, put their heads down, and close their eyes. (It doesn't matter whether they sit on the floor or in chairs.) For the students in this center circle, the entire scene will be played out as if it is the darkest night. Instruct them to stay still and silent.
>
> Next, choose another group of students to form an outer circle. Before they position themselves, give them the text and instruct them to prepare for their roles by highlighting passages, perhaps practicing the way they would perform particular lines by shouting, snarling, menacing, and so on. As they plan for their participation, also let them know that they

may stomp, clap, thump, knock things over, and so forth. Optionally, you can also tell them to rotate the circle when the exercise begins, and to continue circling throughout.

Finally, arrange for a student director to point silently to another member of the outer circle who should say their chosen line. Instruct this person to vary the selection so that the quotes from the text come from all different directions.

Begin the activity with a bell or a sound. The students in the outer circle say the lines as the student director points to them. If everyone follows the directions, the members of the inner circle will hear the voices and sounds coming from all different directions as they sit still and silent in the middle of it all.

Switch groups before you discuss the impact of the exercise.

It is important to note that this is a truly powerful exercise that may be too emotionally charged for some participating students or educators. On one occasion, I created an unfortunate situation where a group of adult learners constituted the inner circle as their tutors read statistics about child abuse. Several people broke down and cried. Allow anyone who might feel threatened to "opt out" and just be an observer.

In the exercise above, the text meaning is heightened in a rather frightening way for the purpose of arousing empathy and replicating the fear triggered by a midnight invasion. Rather than stimulating fear, comprehension for deep or dense text can also be achieved by employing a thoughtful, repetitive, or contemplative treatment of text, such as a philosophical passage. Make sure that the text is not beyond the vocabulary level of the class, even if it is quite challenging to understand. For example, you might draw on Ralph Waldo Emerson's essay, "Self-Reliance." Although the nature of the text is quite different from the strong passage used above, the process of the exercise is similar.

The first step is the same: study the text with the class, reading it through several times. Allow time for all the students to select the text to prepare for their roles. In turn, members of the outer circle highlight the most succinct phrases or words in the text, thereby eliminating portions that detract from their purpose. These highlighted words and phrases become the discourse spoken by the outer circle to the inner circle. Then tell one group of students to form a circle and close their eyes. An upright balance posture is appropriate for this exercise. Instruct them to stay still and silent. The words and phrases may be repeated several times during the exercise in order to heighten the awareness of the meaning. Please see below for an example of how the text might look after highlighting. "There is a time in every man's education when he arrives at the conviction that envy is ignorance; that imitation is suicide; that he must take himself for better, for worse, as his portion; that though the wide universe is full of good,

1) no kernel of nourishing corn can come to him but through his toil bestowed on that plot of ground which is given to him to till.

2) The power which resides in him is new in nature, and none but he knows what that is which he can do, nor does he know until he has tried. Not for nothing one face, one character, one fact, makes much impression on him, and another none.

3) This sculpture in the memory is not without pre-established harmony. The eye was placed where one ray should fall, that it might testify of that particular ray.

4) We but half express ourselves, and are ashamed of that divine idea which each of us represents. It may be safely trusted as proportionate and of good issues, so it be faithfully imparted, but,

5) God will not have his work made manifest by cowards. A man is relieved and gay when he has put his heart into his work and done his best; but what he has said or done otherwise, shall give him no peace. It is a deliverance which does not deliver. In the attempt his genius deserts him; no muse befriends; no invention, no hope."(Ralph Waldo Emerson, "Self-Reliance" from *Essays: First Series,* 1841.)

The teacher may direct the students to move on to another selection of text before discussing the impact of the exercise. The strong effect of working in this manner is that, although this text is very dense, it can actually be appreciated by repetition, reflection and time to digest the meaning.

Exercises that help students expand sensitivity to vocabulary and the intensity of an emotion promote reading comprehension. You can put the words on index cards and have the student order them according to how emotionally charged each of the words is. This addresses the connotative meaning of synonyms rather than the denotative. An example of this follows.

Vocabulary Intensity Scale			
Most Intense	Fearful	Aggressive	Livid
	Apprehensive	Foolhardy	Furious
	Anxious	Courageous	Incensed
Key Word	Shy	Brave	Fuming
	Timid	Bold	Angry
	Bashful	Confident	Cross
	Introverted	Self Assured	Annoyed
Least Intense	Quiet	Secure	Irritated
Note: the level of intensity may be up to interpretation but even that discussion adds to comprehension of these similar words.			

You may want to ask students to act out the meaning of the words with body language and facial expressions or if you have to work silently with pen and paper, then try:

The word	Definition	Antonym	Rendering
wander	To walk around in a directionless way	to stay the course stay on track	

For elementary school children, vocabulary boards with pictures cut out from magazines may be a way for them to learn additional words. They can be given a list, then students write these on index cards, subsequently choosing pictures from magazines that support comprehension. This could become a vocabulary wall and added to throughout the year.

A person with inadequate language skills has no way to express ideas that he/she cannot describe. Weak vocabulary limits thinking because the tools to construct the thought are not available. A weak vocabulary also has a big impact on what is called "Emotional Literacy," or understanding your feelings and the feelings of others. For example, if someone doesn't get the difference between the words and behaviors of the concepts "sophisticated" verses "conceited," she/he might feel insulted by a person who has no such intention.

CHAPTER 16

WHO AM I?

The most basic kind of self-awareness is physical. Developmentally, young kids can use their bodies as anchors to an awareness of their emotions. A common technique is the 'body scan' where the student starts at his toes and systematically tenses and relaxes the muscles. Sometime kids can press their hands together, pushing as hard as they can to feel the tension and then relax. That method can be applied by starting with the toes all the way up to the face. For a subtler kind of awareness, you can ask your students to put their hands on their foreheads. Then you can say:

THE PALM OF MY HAND

Place the palm of your hand on your forehead. Become aware of the skin of your hand touching the warmth of your forehead. Next feel the skin on your forehead *feeling* your palm. Now observe how your will directs what to feel. Who is the voice giving directions? What is the source of that will? How do you observe what you have directed yourself to do?

Middle school children are very busy creating what appears to be a "personality." One might wonder what a "personality is." If it is a collection of ideas about *what I like* and *what I don't like* and that collection forms an identity, then the students are really busy trying out these different roles. It is important for kids to be able to explore and express their talents and temperaments, but if the set of ideas is very self- limiting, it may be necessary for the teacher to remind them that ideas are just mental pictures that one can give energy to and that they are not necessarily true or real.

In the early part of the philosophical training at the Advaita Meditation Center, we are given a model that describes the mind as full of digits or ideas, and our pure consciousness gives these ideas energy that lights them up and we believe them to be real and true. The challenge is to detach from identifying with a particular set of ideas.

When we ask, *who am I*, what can appear in successive layers are the likes and dislikes, habitual emotions and a deep sense of "ahum" or "I am." Often there is just a sense of being alive. Next, there may be an urge to "do" or move and then sometimes a desire for something where the "urge" gets attached to achieving that desire.

The guru Sri Ramanasramam is the source of this practice as I know it, but the exercise is several hundred years old. In his *Who am I?* text, he says that:

> *"For all thoughts the source is the 'I' thought. The mind will merge only by Self-enquiry 'Who am I?' The thought 'Who am I?' will destroy all other thoughts and finally kill itself also. If other thoughts arise, without trying to complete them, one must enquire to whom did this thought arise. What does it matter how many thoughts arise? As each thought arises one must be watchful and ask to whom is this thought occurring. The answer will be 'to me". If you enquire 'Who am I?' the mind will*

return to its source (or where it issued from). The thought which arose will also submerge. As you practice like this more and more, the power of the mind to remain as its source is increased."

STUDENT VERSION (USE WHO OR WHAT)

Who am I? Am I my clothes, my family, my home, my friends, what I own?

If not, then, who am I?

Am I what I do? the kind of music I like, my work, my talents, the sports, and games?

Then if not, who am I?

Am I this body, these organs, these senses of perception – the ability to hear, see, taste, feel, smell?

Then if not, Who am I?

Am I this blood coursing through veins, this breath, the food I eat, the chemical interchange of blood and digestion? Am I these ideas, this set of likes and dislikes, the subtle shifts in attitude, my intelligence?

Then if not who am I?

Am I these feelings of awareness extending infinitely in and infinitely out? Am I awakeness?

Then if not, who am I? Am I this witness, the pure indescribable, the one, unmoving, timeless, boundless, having no inside, no outside, limitless consciousness?

Who am I?

The adolescent brain may be really challenged by this experiment because the art of introspection does not fully develop until about age 26, and even then maturity seems to continue to increase. A warm up to "Who am I" is the following exercise:

WHO REMEMBERS

When you were quite young you had a moment that was important to you. Think of something you remember clearly that meant something to you. Fill your mind with the details of that moment. The time of day, how you felt, who was there, what was going on, and so forth. Be in that place for a minute or two. Make the memory bright in your mind. Feel the sense, the trace it left on you.

Now come back to yourself in the present. Consider that your body is not the same. Every cell in your body has changed. The blood that flows through your veins has changed. Your emotional self has grown, developed and changed. Your intellect and mind have matured. Now contemplate: what is it in you that remembers that moment? Who is this that is the same you that witnessed that moment in time? this you that doesn't change with the passing of years? Rest with that for a moment.

Pause.

What is it in you that remembers? What is the witness of that moment that holds this in mind? Is the you of now the same as the you in your memory?

It is important that a sense of security and control develops in the students. Although most things change, there is something about life that is permanent, deep, immutable and invulnerable. That cannot be something physical, nor could it be described spiritually, but most people realize that a sense of his/her most essential self exists and doesn't change. This is a longer, subtler exercise in the observation of the mechanics of the mind based on the recognition that a "core" or essential self is unchanged from childhood through adulthood.

Think about your own experiences. How authentic and real were you at 12, 16, 21? I recall a great deal of defensiveness and confusion about values, how to behave, morality. The confusion was a reaction to my parents' restrictions but that reaction was just as mechanical as thoughtlessly living life in the same way as the previous generation. Wouldn't it be nice to grow up "free" from trying to figure out how to be "cool"? Emerson said, we "*but half express ourselves, and are ashamed of that divine idea which each of us represents.*" ("Self-Reliance.") So the "who am I?" exercise is getting in touch with the essence or most basic part of yourself.

Many years ago, in an attempt to get me to sit still, my spiritual teacher asked me to pretend to play the role of the guru in a ceremony. During the exercise, each person in the group was to come up to the guru and bow. I think they also placed flowers or fruit in front of the guru. Since the tutor told me I couldn't move at all, I hoped that by channeling the guru's energy, I could be very still. As it sometimes happens in spiritual exercises, the symbolism of the moment was blessed and energized. As each of the participants came up to the guru, what I saw was that each of them had a special trait, talent or some aspect of themselves that was a manifestation of the divine.

As the first person approached, I saw: "A love of beauty, precision and careful arrangement in the home." In another, I saw: "industry" and willingness to work with long endurance. In another, a sweet, humble woman, I saw "magnificence." Her integrity, honesty, generosity were spiritually "magnificent." These impressions were not imaginings, predictable or vague, but rather insights about these people that captured the essences of what they were here in order to express, in this creation. Everyone who participated was deeply moved, and those qualities seen in these people linger to this day.

The point of telling you this is that I believe each child has an "essence," a talent, a divine spark that she/he is here to manifest; moreover that essence is uniquely a part of them. If you can find and encourage them to grow, train, and nourish this gift, it will be profoundly fulfilling and useful to that student and the world.

CHAPTER 17

TURBO FOCUS

TikTik Shaa: What a wonderful word! What a wonderful concept! One of its meanings is to tolerate minor physical and mental discomforts in order to concentrate. A word in English that adequately describes it is "Laser-Power" or "Turbo Focus": it means focus on one thing only, ignoring all distractions. I eagerly espouse this as a "super power" for kids. While it is true that some conditions are optimal, if one allows every little thing to dominate the consciousness and then uses that as a way to avoid work, nothing will get done. There will always be a distraction of one kind or another. The itch on the nose, the noise in the hall, and the absence of perfect music will always be an issue.

A form of procrastination that middle school students frequently engage in is, "The conditions are not just right," "I need this or that in order to work," "I need a certain kind of music to concentrate on my math," "I have to work with my best friend," "I need a table that looks out the window," and so on.

It is unlikely that the student will accept an explanation from you such as, "Oh you are just allowing that to distract you," so you might say, "Oh I can see how that might bother you," and then say: "How about if we try for the next 10 minutes to concentrate on your work in spite of this irritation? Try to develop your super power of Turbo Focus."

After a bit, you can ask, "how is it going? Are you able to focus in spite of the distraction?" Then you offer a challenge: "let's see if you can get your work done up to this particular page before we do anything about the irritation." Offer the analogy of the Emergency Medical Technicians who have to work under extremely tense and distracting conditions, yet they can focus on the patient with laser light attention. "Try to show me your strength by focusing on this one thing." Attention is like a muscle; it gets stronger every time you practice controlling it. Attention is also directly proportional to the amount you learn. Full attention means that the brain will receive and synthesize the information available.

Focus on Students

Learning Disabled students often struggle to find ways to absorb new material. When resistance is very high and the child is stressed, it can sometimes be the result of a mental and emotional "freeze." That is the time to give them a "magic feather," as it were. It can be a stone to rub with their fingers, an encouraging phrase like "I can do this" or a mantra like "Shanti." They can say "Focus" to their minds or "Stop" to the negative ideas. They might say, "My mind is an instrument for my use." Give them a bridge to get over that wall of static that is blocking their aptitude. They are temporarily like a "flooded" engine and need a break to regain the spark to move efficiently.

A competitive student may like to have a stopwatch which can be set to go off when the designated amount of time on task is reached. You can present this as a challenge to the group also. As teachers, we, too, often find that we have to work on acceptance of the situation "as is" before presenting it!

Another way of looking at this kind of tolerance is "allowing" things to be as they are without requiring that the circumstances change to suit your preferences. The wisdom in this acceptance is that it doesn't matter that you prefer a different situation; each individual has to cope with the current, real environment. The only way to effect any change is to deal with the reality, as it exists. Some people call this acceptance of the "flow" of life. A phrase that encourages that acceptance is "allow things to be as they are."

You might have to wait until a student is ready to learn a particular skill instead of trying to fit him/her into a schedule. Year after year, I tried to teach students the value of planning, writing a project in the agenda book, blocking out times for rough drafts, editing and final copy. Year after year, some students would refuse to try it and then suddenly, around their 16th birthday, I would overhear them say to a younger student, "Yo, just write it down, dude." When I questioned them, I could never get a clear answer on why there was this sudden change. They were just growing up.

Another way to dismantle a cycle of negative thinking is to use the "shower of encouragement" method. In Los Angeles, California, in 2007, Shelly Stockwell-Nicholas, President of the *International Hypnosis Federation* and author of over 15 books and CDs, presented the "All About You" hypnosis class that used this strategy to combat negative thinking or the blocking of the natural flow to creativity. When a person is trying to concentrate on a particular task and gets stuck in negative thoughts, this kind of chatter is called "circling thoughts." What characterizes a circling thought is that it is often a collection of half sentences, phrases, and words that overlap in a kind of cacophony of criticism: *Who do you think you are, you're as dumb as you look, you never could do math, you stink at spelling, why are you so slow, you're just not smart enough to learn this.*

These words may or may not have been said to us as children or are not remembered clearly but come up as a clutch in the heart or a binding in the throat. This interference to directing our energy to where we want it is like a wall of static between two radio stations. Depending on how severe the trauma was, a trigger may set off a "trance-like" state where the person has to lose touch with the present in order to survive.

As a child, my dyslexia showed up mostly in handwriting. I would reverse letters, drop endings, make a terrible scrawl and forget how to spell simple words. In second grade, I was asked to write the color "red" on the chalk board. What I wrote was: wred, wrede, read, rede, wread. The teacher/nun mocked me. "Image that! She can't even spell the color RED." I sat down deeply ashamed.

About 45 years later, I was asked to address envelopes with a fountain pen at a philosophy mail-out exercise. The pressure to do it correctly, evenly and with no errors the first time threw me into a trance state. My friend, Zoe, had to call my name several times because I was reliving my second-grade moment, staring into space, frozen in toxic shame. The trigger was a minor incident. Imagine what it can be like for a child who has had more severe emotional attacks. So what is the antidote? One strategy is to reverse the negative sayings with positive ones and to set up the experience so that the voices sound similar to head chatter and come from all directions. This is "a shower of encouragement."

Our team in the hypnosis class worked with a woman who had an issue about not being able to write down her ideas and thoughts. She had been told by a teacher in the 3rd grade that she couldn't write and, in any case, what she wanted to say wasn't worth writing. The team, a group of four women, asked her to describe her experiences in detail, and then we wrote down phrases that were the positive counterpart such as:

Your ideas are important and worth sharing.

There is a wonderful flow to what you have to say.

You can express your thoughts well.

You are a talented writer.

Then, three of us stood near her as she sat down in a relaxed state, and we showered her with encouragement, praise and compliments. We poured this on for about four minutes, overlapping, interrupting each other and mirroring what was heard in the mind. It doesn't matter if the statements have not yet become true. With practice, they will become true and will effectively replace the limiting ones with expansive ideas.

CHAPTER 18

FLOW

One of the meditation images that helps people relax is to think of their mind as if it were a big blue sky. They can picture that image internally. Then, think of the thoughts that arise as clouds going across the big blue sky. The thought temporarily covers the blue but does not affect it. Try this script or your own variation.

MIND LIKE A BIG BLUE SKY

When you are feeling especially peaceful, sometimes your mind is like a big blue sky. It is vast, clear, clean, open and limitless. If a thought appears, it is just a little cloud floating across your blue-sky mind. It forms, shifts, drifts and disappears from view. If rain clouds appear, the weather gathers, releases and passes. Whatever passes over your blue-sky mind does not change its color. It is blue no matter what passes over it.

[You can also add: your emotions are like the weather, changing over the course of the day, sometimes grey, sometime bright, but never changing the essential you.)

Another image that is frequently used to help students recognize that change is natural, continuous and ceaseless is the idea of a brook or river flowing to the ocean. The thoughts (or attachments) are like sticks and leaves stuck in the rocks. Eventually, they move down river from the pressure of the water.

Another Flow-type script is to allow things to be as they are while you, as the sun, witness them. You may try the following exercise. Feel free to add your own details depending on the amount of time you have.

BE THE SUN

Have the students stand and put their hands together, palms touching about mid-chest level. Say: "Visualize the sun on the horizon over a deep blue ocean at dawn. At first, it is just a line of blue light, but gradually it rises up and becomes more like a circle. Follow its movement and become the sun. (Show the student how to raise your hands up slowly and stretch high as in the Yoga exercise, the Salutation to the Sun.) As it rises, the earth begins to take on light and color. The sky color changes from a blue green to light blue. You, the sun, (let your arms make a wide arc) bless the earth with your heat and life force, gently warming everything you see and everything you pass over. Because of your light and heat, everything grows. Then, as the day ends, you drift back down behind the mountains until only a rosy glow is left and the shimmering night stars reappear. Put your hands back together, palms touching. (Do this as slowly as possible.)

CHAPTER 19

PRACTICING CONTENTMENT

There are many scripts devoted to a sense of satisfaction and completeness. The premise of this is that when we are our most authentic selves, a layer of worry, agitation or unhappiness is not covering this real self; we are naturally happy. It is the a-priori assumption in the Advaita tradition that our natural state is happy, and, if we are experiencing misery, it is caused by the choices we make. One of the most challenging tenants of Advaita is that misery is a choice not a necessity.

In order to practice contentment, do the Stop exercise and then ask the student to recall a time when he/she was happy, not in a jazzy, excited, hopped-up way, but quietly and contentedly happy. Tell them that the class will practice a moment of contentment.

CONTENTMENT

Ask your students: "Recreate in your minds every detail of a moment of contentment. Remember the time of day, the reason you were happy, and the place where you were." Next ask them to "concentrate on this sense of completeness, place it right in the middle of your heart, and allow it to grow while you breathe deeply."

Then say to them, "You are whole, perfect and complete." Say it three times, and then add, "Right here, and right now."

Rest in this peace for one to five minutes. Allow a few questions and discussion. Ask the students to practice saying the words if they want to at other times during the day: "I am whole, perfect and complete."

A variation of this exercise is to say to your students: "You are beingness, consciousness and bliss." That is translated from the Sanskrit: *Sat Chit Ananda. Sat* means transcendent beingness, *Chit* is the groundedness of our being within the source of love or loving awareness, and *Ananda* is happiness without a cause or object.

If you are uncomfortable with these strong descriptions, use a triad of virtues—"you are truth, intelligence and goodness," or "...goodness, honesty and industriousness." Usually, it doesn't do any harm to give a compliment, whereas a "criticism" tends to bind and limit our vision of what is possible. (Reference:http://silentawareness.org/teachings/satchitananda.html)

It is important to note that philosophically, the meaning of self here is not "my human self, with my bundle of likes/dislikes is whole, perfect and complete." It means "my God-self, the light within me, the essence of me that transcends limitations is that which is whole, perfect and complete. When

I acknowledge that I am a manifestation of that which is the source, I am whole, perfect and complete." The wise ones would tell us that the human self is the illusion and the divine self is the reality.

The teacher can adapt the virtues to the situation. For instance, if the students are trying to work collaboratively but are annoying each other, you might say, "I am co-operative, patient and industrious."

Here are some alternative triads:

- *Dependable, truthful and kind*
- *Aware, confident and courteous*
- *Reasonable, accepting and considerate*
- *Tactful, persistent and industrious*
- *Attentive, creative and industrious*
- *Fair, flexible and good*
- *Honest, industrious, and kind*
- *Generous, perceptive and careful*

CHAPTER 20

WHAT HAPPENED HERE?

When you attempt to increase a student's awareness of self, time and the depth of history are important factors. Young people have little context in which to judge the relative goodness or badness of their behaviors or of an event. You can interject a quick sense of time by asking: "if you were living here 100 years ago, how would you get to school?" Or, "what did people do to entertain themselves 50 years ago or 100 years ago? What did people wear then and how did they get that clothing?"

When you have a chance to do a more extended exercise, it is recommended that you set aside about five to ten minutes. Have the kids do a regular Stop and then begin by asking the class to respond silently to these questions:

TIME

Become aware of this room and this space and this time. What is around us? The people, the machines, the light, etc. Let yourself relax and allow your mind to visualize and hear. Image what was happening here when your parents were young. What did the people look like? Was the building new? (After each question, pause for about 15 seconds to allow the student to create an image.) What was here 50 years ago? Was the school here? What kind of land was here? Was there a forest or desert?

What was here 200 years ago? How did the people live? If they went to school, how did they get there? What did they eat and do every day? How did they heat their houses? What was hardship for them? What was pleasure?

Think about land, mountains and rivers as they existed here 300 years ago. What and who lived here? What did they eat? How did they get that food? What were they wearing? What were the animals and plants like?

Try 500 years ago, 1000, 10,000, 1,000,000 years. The Paleozoic era, Mesozoic era, etc.

After a sustained silence of about 2 minutes or so, ask them gently to come back through the ages, gradually becoming present to room awareness. You can ask them to draw or discuss what they thought with each other or share out loud if there is time.

A very successful math/science challenge related to time done at the Parker school was to have the children do a physical representation of geological time. This exercise uses physical distance to symbolize time. Children used hallways, walkways, stairwells, basketball courts and segmented them off to designate millions of years in earth's history.

This activity was much enjoyed because the measuring and labeling required running around outdoors and a good amount of discussion. Any time you can have students "walk through" an experience or experiment, more learning is happening because they are physically and mentally performing something: thinking, sensing, seeing.

CHAPTER 21

AN ATTITUDE OF GRATITUDE

One of the misconceptions that youngsters have is a sense of independence or separateness from the rest of the world. They believe that they are functioning freely, and their actions have no impact on others nor do they depend on others. Sometimes this develops into a surly attitude that sounds like "you can't tell me what to do because I don't need you." So, in order to have a more realistic take on their place in the world, one of the exercises is: "Where does this shirt come from?" You can do this with food, toys, objects or clothing, but the important aspect of it is that the child recognizes his place in the larger chain of events.

GRATITUDE

Find an item of clothing that you are wearing: a shirt, a sweater. Now have a classmate check the label in the back: where does this item come from? (Often China or the Pacific Rim). Now let's stop, close your eyes and follow my voice. Think about the time that you were first given this shirt. Mentally acknowledge this gift to that person. Go back and think about who hung or folded the shirt in the store. Think about the person who unloaded the box or bundle of shirts from the truck. Imagine the warehouse, the central distribution place where the shirts were unpacked from huge crates and put in boxes to go to the store. Think about the place that the huge crates came from. Perhaps it was a dock in Long beach, California, where giant barges loaded six-high with railroad car-sized containers held the shirts. Think about the person who ran the crane with the claw that moved the container from the barge to the dock. Imagine the ship's captain and the crew who steered the ship over to the US. Think about the workers (in China or Thailand) who loaded the crates onto the ship. Think about the people who packed the materials in the factory where the shirts were made. Think about the person who sewed your shirt in the factory. Think about the person who cut the material to make your shirt. Think about the bolts of material being woven by the machines and the thread being spun and the workers who watched over them. Think about the raw materials, the balls of cotton that had to be carded and cleaned. Think about the farmer who grew the cotton and planted the seed. Think about the rain, the sunshine and the earth in which the seed grew. Think about the source of the sun, earth, and rain.

Let this sink in for a while – the number of steps, the number of people that it takes to bring you one item of clothing.

I had a student say after this exercise, "God made my pants!" which was lovely. But even if the kids do not get that kind of insight, it is important that they have a glimpse of how many people it takes to make and deliver just one item to their lives. Our whole lives depend on the good will – and labor– of others. So the idea that we are independent is foolish. Everything comes to us from the actions of others, and nature itself is a "gift" from the Absolute.

Often a kind of skepticism and arrogance arises in students during the second half of their seventh grade school year. I have seen thousands of kids develop this. This stage lasts until June, but seems disappear by the next fall when they begin the eighth grade. Kids are testing their limits with authority figures and being as willful as they can be. When they hit this stage, I often tell the group that they are going through a phase. I ask the class if anyone knows a two-year-old, and then follow up by asking, "You know how obnoxious a two-year-old can be? For instance, when they're tired, but they insist they're not tired and don't need a nap? Or when they've taken a cookie and you ask them if they took it, but they insist that they didn't even though they have crumbs all over their face?" Most students recognize the truth of this description. So then, I go on, "You may not realize it now, but you are the teenaged equivalent of a two-year-old. You may be feeling all big and bad but you don't have a clue yet about how to behave. Therefore, keep two words in mind. You can either 'Differ,' which means you can challenge everything your teachers say, or you can 'Defer,' which means you'll wait and see if what they say works or is truthful and for now just listen and try it out." Most kids can relate to this.

The principle here is that I, in my current state, do not know everything, so I can listen, try something out and see if it works: That is deference.

There is an

'I'

in "Differ"

as in "I differ."

But when you take out the 'I'

you have an E as in

"I defer"

or "I consider everyone."

CHAPTER 22

PROVE IT TO ME: IS ATTENTION REAL ENERGY?

This exercise is a great deal of fun, and if the teacher wants about 10 minutes of silent time, it's a way to get it. I start off by asking, "Have you ever noticed how when you are riding around in your car and you take a good look at someone in the next car, they turn and look at you? Why is that? How can they 'feel' you looking at them? What kind of energy is transmitted across the road, through the glass, that causes the person to turn suddenly and look you directly in the eye as if you poked them?" Most kids have had this kind of experience. I explain it by saying that when you pay attention to someone, your attention has actual energy that the other person can feel.

You can also try other games with energy such as, "Throwing a ball of light." Students can create an imaginary ball by holding their palms close but not touching and generate the "electric" field between their hands. They can then toss the ball of light up and catch it or toss it back and forth. Next, they can toss it to each other across the room. They can pretend it's heavy or light, flat or oval.

Another sensitivity game is to "mirror" each other. Two students face each other. Decide on the leader and try to have the two mirror each other's slow motions without chatter. The idea is to move in parallel to each other as if your partner is the mirror. This tests powers of observation and muscle control and also the sense of unity. I suspect that the urge to trick someone into going in the wrong direction is almost irresistible. The result will be much giggling.

ATTENTION IS ENERGY

Tell the group to line up on two sides of a big table. Next, write down the name of one student who is sitting on the opposite side. Everyone closes their eyes and is very quiet, as all students on the one side reads the name silently and then passes along the card.

They then concentrate and stare at that designated student in the line opposite them. The students in the other line are to remain with eyes closed until they feel the "pressure" of the stare. Then they open their eyes to check to see if they are "the one" being stared at.

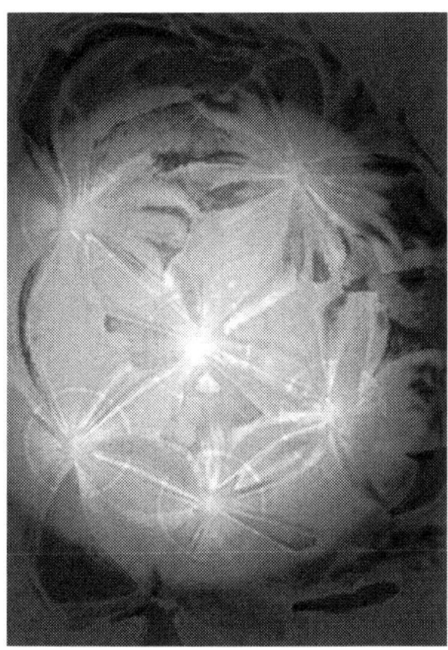

Try the following (a longer "proof" of the effectiveness of meditation can be conducted as a before and after trial using the standard scientific method). You will need two comparable mazes, two word lists of ten random words, a set of writing prompts, paper and writing tools.

Day 1

MAZE

On the first day, you give the student a drawn labyrinth/maze. Try to make it challenging enough for it to take at least one minute to figure out. The teacher can place stop-watches around or keep putting the time on the board. Have the students write their time on the top of their paper.

MEMORIZATION

Next you say: I am going to read off ten random words. I will read the list twice. After I finish, write down as many of them as you can remember. (It is important that the list has no pattern.)

WRITING FLUENCY

Next, hand out writing prompts and time them for 5 minutes. The amount of writing they do in that 5 minutes is considered to be "writing fluency." Have them count the words in their story and write that down.

Day 2

Have the student sit quietly for a full five minutes. They can:

breathe

use a word

stare at a focus point

listen to the furthest sound

Go through the same set of tasks: the Maze, the Word list and the Writing fluency. Follow the same procedure as the first trial. Listening to music doesn't work because some music is not appropriate to the exercise and it cannot really be monitored; also, music for the group imposes that music on everyone.

This exercise is almost guaranteed to improved performance for two reasons, the first is these task are now familiar and the second is a quiet time before work... really does help. It might be fun to get the percent of improvement one each task.

People feel each other's energies, and toxic attitudes such as gossip, criticism, shaming or shunning can create a hostile and unfriendly atmosphere. That makes the job of the teacher doubly hard because it requires that she/he also masters her/his attitudes and thoughts as well as words and behavior.

As the team leader, your warmth and encouragement is a powerful tool. There is more on this topic in the chapter on Social Capital.

THE SILENT MESSAGE

Have the class send one or two people out into the hallway. Then have the class throw dice; an odd number might mean a "positive" vibe and an even number might be a "negative" vibe. The class has to choose whether they are going to send loving or hateful thoughts to those student outside when they return to class. In addition, the class cannot say anything or show through body language or facial expressions what they are thinking. Take a few turns and observe if people can sense kindness or hostility. Follow up by a discussion of the effects of feeling rejected or accepted. Be careful that you don't put an "at risk" student in an embarrassing situation.

CHAPTER 23

COLORING, DRAWING AND CALLIGRAPHY

Mandala kits are on the market and consist of a variety of beautiful designs which can be colored in with markers, pencils or crayons. The students get to choose the ones they want and then spend some time filling then in with color. This is usually a welcomed, calming activity after high-stress times such as taking an important test or pre-vacation jitters.

A Mandala can also be hand-drawn by using themes or symbols that are meaningful to the kids or by outlining mathematical geometric shapes. The pattern can grow outward or inward. Some children will enjoy creating their own designs on the computer and then sharing them with others. Neverthless, the real effectiveness of this exercise is based on focusing on the tip of the coloring tool and slowly working around the Mandala. It is meant to be a thoughtful and well-paced exercise. Students generally love it. Mandalas have also been used as objects for contemplation. This exercise essentially means looking at the Mandala for a time, absorbing a clear impression in great detail and then bringing the image into your heart.

Another standard practice is to imagine a color as a ball of light and concentrate on that. Visual sense is also used in the following practice:

> Tell the student you are going to practice using their visual memory. Have a still-life arrangement on a table where they can see it and give everyone drawing materials. Next ask the student to study the still-life and try to memorize every detail of it. Then cover it up with a cloth. Give the student about four to five minutes to draw what they remember. Compare the still-life to their drawings and share observations.

Another focusing exercise concerns observing "negative space," an old art technique and a bit of a mind-boggler. Instead of drawing an object with lines as the outline of an object, take the side of the chalk or crayon and use it to color the space around the object. Everything around the object becomes a shadow and the light within the object is dark (opposite).

A recent hobby I have tried is called the ZenTangle (information is available online). Here is an example. The exercise is to follow any original line carefully, but if it changes, then go with the new shape. It is supposed to "still" the mind because it requires sustained concentration on the point of a fined-tipped pen. This is very similar to calligraphy exercises but with shapes instead of words.

The squares below represent sticky note squares, but a tangle can be done on any sized paper as well.

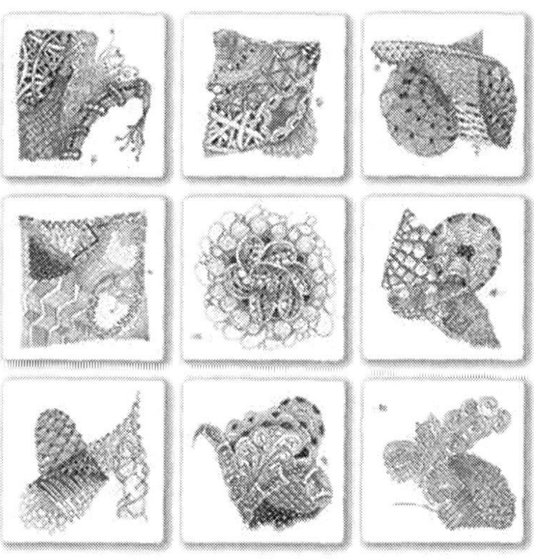

Tell the student that you are going to practice using visual memory.

Place a still-life in the center of the table

Flower, objects and so on. Ask them to study it for one or two minutes and try to notice every detail of the arrangement.

Then you cover up the arrangement with a cloth and have the student try to draw it from memory. After drawing for a time, uncover the still-life and notice how it differs from the memory. You might ask why they think that happens. Share your observations.

Some educators recommend writing in script (cursive) as a faster, more flowing way to get the ideas out and down; many students in the US, however, don't learn script well and don't practice it often. It may soon become obsolete and they may not be able to read it.

Bring in a sheet of the cursive letters, both capitals and small letters, and hand out a copy for each student. Then on the type of paper that has a dotted line half above and half below the main line, ask them to write their name beautifully. Next, they can use each letter of their name to begin a new word that they then copy, going down the page. For example:

B – brilliant

R – ridiculous

I – intelligent

A – authentic

N – nerd

- Write a inspirational quote on the board that they copy
- Have them choose a quote to copy from a list
- Have them create a poster to hang in their rooms for inspiration
- Write words or lines of letters with f, g, j, h, z , x, y
- Make straight lines down a clean page
- Make connected circles or letters
- Try writing with the non-dominant hand
- Write by looking only in a mirror
- Write categories in cursive such as names of cities in your state

Tell your students that the purpose is not how wobbly or beautiful the writing looks, but the ability to keep the attention right where the lead or ink leaves the pencil tip and to return to that point again and again. Once in a while you might have a student comment on how the writing goes off when there is a distracting thought. If a student allows herself to go very deep, she might remember the original moment when she first learned to write. She also might remember some trauma or painful experience. If the student does experience some discomfort, you can tell her it is a natural part of healing to remember and release. They can breathe through it.

Don't forget writing numbers too. They can be written on graph paper inside the squares or made into patterns to fill in the tiny squares. Other fine motor control practices are sewing, knitting, crocheting, sorting beads into separate boxes with tweezers.

ILLUMINATION PRACTICE

From time to time, we need to encourage ourselves with an appropriate quote or aphorism that addresses our particular challenge. This exercise is called "Illumination." Have the kids pick a quote, aphorism or homily that is meaningful to them, something that gets them excited, a challenge. It should be a quote or saying that is the first thing they see in the morning and sets the tone for the day. It needs to be a worthwhile saying, not just a popular idiom. When I was in graduate school, the first thing I chose to see was a poster that said CAN DO! I know that is less than elegant but it did provide a little juice for the day. On the finest paper available, with their most elegant calligraphy, have them copy the quote with the intention to post it where they see it often.

Some students feel quite insecure about their drawing talents. An alternative way to an artistic activity that does not depend on hand eye co-ordination is making a collage. A collage can symbolize the aspirations of a group, be an interpretation of a novel or represent the passions of an individual.

All that is needed is some stiff paper or cardboard for backing, glue and a variety of magazines. Try to have magazines that represent a variety of interests including cars, food, sports, animals, architecture, gardening, ecology, politics, as well as fashion. Collages can represent current interests and also support goals and desires for the future.

When my son was 17, I made him a collage that documented his interests in Islamic studies and writing, among other topics. The fact that it celebrated his interests, instead of imposing my wishes, was a comfort when he brought this to college. Since this kind of artwork can be a validation of someone's personality, it might work nicely as an end of the year gift for students to give to each other as a way of verifying that they know each other well and are developing connections.

For the science teacher, the following is useful when you need a nature observation connection. Instruct the class that you are going to study four square inches of earth by observing the details and zooming in on the small. It can be connected to writing/drawing exercises that encourage students to be precise and detailed in their descriptions of the physical world. At first, this procedure may seem very bland, but after a minute of looking, a student might find a fragment of a brown oak leaf, a pine needle, white seed, green hemlock leaf, brown dirt, green grass, dried hay-like grass, an ant, curled baby clover, etc. With a little more time, even more detail might become apparent. The important thing is noticing the life that we so frequently overlook.

Four Square Inches: Give each student a 16-inch piece of string. Tell them that they are going outside, and that they are to place the string on the ground in a square (or circular) shape with the ends touching. Their shape will provide an approximately four-square-inch area for them to observe. Once they create their observation area, they are to draw all the items within it and label them.

A length of plain cotton string is a great game starter. I was surprised when, during a moment when the students needed an activity, I passed out string and taught them how to play "cat's cradle." They loved it. This game requires attention to the placement of the fingers at the crosses and, because the person who holds the string has to teach the learner with verbal directions only, it encourages clear communication. This game never seems to fail to delight the 7th graders as a learning and teaching activity.

CHAPTER 24

SACRED WORDS MANTRAS

One mystic tradition teaches that words are the "causal level creation": when the object is named, it contains the essence of that object. This tradition holds that creation was spoken into existence and that the first word spoken was **OM**. Beings come into existence because God speaks their names. In this view, words have real meaning. The objects exist in name and form only, and, in reality, everything is the same substance but assumes different shapes, densities, states of growth and decay. A word can be very powerful; a name that contains the nature and the vibration state of the object, but that requires that the language in which it is said is the pure or cosmic language. It may be that the purest form of a word is pre-verbal. This tradition indicates that Sanskrit is closest to this original language.

When people repeat a word or mantra, it is important that the word be harmonious and healthy for that particular being. Because teachers would not be permitted to initiate children into a formal meditation practice and give them specific mantras, let the children choose their own favorite word and ask them to be careful about what they choose. It should have a positive meaning, have a sound that is soothing and be easy to repeat internally. (The syllable **OM** is generally not recommended because the wise suggest that it be reserved for people who are committed to following a spiritual path in monastic life.)

Here are some of the words we used:

One	Shalom (peace in Hebrew)	Serenity	*Shanti* (peace in Sanskrit)
Peace	One of the names of God from their tradition	Calm	*Inshalla* (Arabic *in shā' Allāh- God willing)*
Joy	Unity	Tranquility	Harmony
Bliss	Light and love	*So Hum* (*I am* in Sanskrit)	*Sat, Chit, Ananda* (truth, consciousness, bliss in Sanskrit)

Have the student chose whatever word they want to repeat internally. The quick repetition of the word is called *Japa,* and it is supposed to interrupt the flow of mechanical thoughts. However, it is not necessary to continue repeating the word quickly but rather to let it slow down or flow as it will. You can have the student do this exercise for about 4 minutes or for as long as it is comfortable for him. I did have a young man who thought it would be "cool" if he repeated the word "death." He said afterwards that it made him quite uncomfortable.

An alternative is listening to music or sound that induces a tranquil state and even breathing. The next section, "Music," offers several exercises for using music in the classroom.

CHAPTER 25

MUSIC

Most students love music. Good music is uplifting. It is not a matter of taste, but of how music can be used. Because of its regular rhythm and harmonics, baroque music is considered to be the best option to support sustained concentration. Music is like an auditory fence. When the attention wanders or the mind needs a little break, it is easy to stay in the area if there is music in the background. We stop, listen a while and return to work. Music tends to blot out other distractions that are more likely to trigger the mind wandering off into the world at large. Music organizes the brain to create alpha rhythms which are consistent with creative thought.

One musical exercise for students is to focus on a single instrument, a violin or guitar, for instance. You could call that, "Zoom in." They might listen for the silence between the notes or the silence from which the sound arises. Often a single harmonic tone runs throughout an entire piece. It is that thrum that you can hear in the background. Keith Richards, from the Rolling Stones, talked about deliberately setting up that note in his own music. This gives a sustained power to the song which can be found by a "Zoom Out" or relaxed kind of listening. (*Footnote Life*, a memoir by Richards written with the assistance of journalist, James Fox, published in October 2010, chronicles Richards' love, complex understanding and manipulation of music.)

An interesting correlation to Vedanta is that the universe is described as "singing." When we are very still, there is an awareness of the substrata to life and sounds arising from *Akasha.* It is extremely subtle but I myself have heard an *aahhhh* rolling up the mountainside or when the inner view appears to open up into infinite space. Two close replications of that sound are the continuous sound of *Aaah* or *Om* as members of the meditation groups enter in turn, and Gregorian chants.

Another option is the singing of the vowels of the alphabet. The vowels in Sanskrit are called *Spota* or the "shining ones." The tradition describes Sanskrit as the words meaning what they do, in the creative sense. When the word is spoken, it creates what the word describes. I have never seen Sanskrit create a thing, but I have seen it create emotions and insight. At the Rudolf Steiner Waldorf schools, teachers are known to sing the vowel and add dance movements to it, known as Eurhythmy.

If you happen to be musically talented and trained to use instruments, curricula with music can easily be woven into History, English, and Social Studies. Although lyrics may not apply to Science and Math, you can certainly apply the way notes are created, whole notes being halved, quartered and eighthed. Rhythms and metric of beat can also be included. Rounds are also effective. Two easy ones are "Dona Nobis Pacem" and "Happiness Runs" by Donovan.

Neurologically, music causes a different reaction from the spoken or written word. Singing and listening create a potent arousal of emotions. Most of the time, we are only aware of ourselves and the people in our immediate lives.

Sometimes that circle of awareness can be tiny, but singing opens the heart as well as the lungs. Singing words that expand the sense of self to include others in this world makes us aware that everyone (dare I say everything) deserves care and consideration, as do we. The emotions awakened by singing can create strong connections to the principals of truth, justice and freedom.

Many folk songs, notably quite a few sung by *Peter, Paul, and Mary*, evoke a sense of unity and brotherhood. Take a look at the lyrics of the following:

"See What Tomorrow Brings" 1965

The words to "Because All Men are Brothers" Bach/Glazer- Amrita Music Corp. ASCAP:

Because all men are brothers wherever men may be One Union shall unite us forever proud and free No tyrant shall defeat us, no nation strike us down All men who toil shall greet us the whole wide world around.

My brothers are all others forever hand in hand Where chimes the bell of freedom there is my native land My brother's fears are my fears yellow white or brown My brother's tears are my tears the whole wide world around.

Let every voice be thunder, let every heart beat strong Until all tyrants perish our work shall not be done Let not our memories fail us the lost year shall be found Let slavery's chains be broken the whole wide world around.

Young people often go through a period when they like angry, raucous, chaotic noise. My son went through a phase where his agitation was so intense that he enjoyed loud, brash, cacophonous sounds. So a music exercise is an opportunity to introduce the idea that certain kinds of music have certain effects on our physical /emotional selves.

An experiment designed to promote an understanding of

THE AFFECT OF MUSIC

Arrange to have 3 or 4 samples of vastly different music and then tell the class that they are going to make marks on a clean surface , like a sheet of butcher paper that will indicate their emotional response to the music. The marks can be lines, squiggles, dots, jabs. slashes, waves or whatever. Have different stations around the room where some student are listening and making marks while others are observing. Have the students who are responding to the music keep their eyes closed or be blindfolded so that they are not copying each other. Play each sample in turn and put aside the responses. At the end of the listening portion of the exercise, put all the samples up at grouped into the categories of the sample played. Observe the kind of lines that student made.

Ask them to say what emotion the lines suggest. Are they calm, agitated, happy and so on. Share out what this means in terms of what choices they make in their listening menu. Should they listen to heavy metal to do their homework? Does reggae make you energetic ? Does classical music help you concentrate?

Some quick practices are:

1. Have them tap out the rhythm with their finger tips

2. Find the melody and learn to sing that

3. Find the Harmonic tone in the piece

4. Identify the emotions that arise when listening.

Soryuforall, who is an expert on the use of music, suggested that students can Zoom out and pay attention to all the sounds of a song or to zoom in on a single instrument. They can also focus on the silence between the notes .

CHAPTER 26

EXERCISE AND MOVEMENT

What do a country line dance, a martial arts "kata, a T'ai Chi exercise and yoga have in common? They all require bilateral movement. Anytime the brain is required to move the opposite sides of the body in different directions, the body develops coordination and balance. This kind of movement usually requires a conscious effort to control the muscles, and body awareness is enhanced. Exercise stimulates the brain, which increases aptitude for learning in general. Furthermore, exercise requiring bilateral movement is even more potent because it helps students develop specific pathways in the brain that deal with dexterity (Kurtz).

Focus on Students

In middle school, "klutzy" students often become the target of teasing, whereas poor students with good athletic skills can be assured of social acceptance based on their coordination. If it is possible to include targeted exercises as part of an Individualized Education Plan (IEP) to improve the coordination of learning disabled kids, it will go a long way toward improving not only their self-esteem, but also their chances for social inclusion.

Body movement practices based on washing machine agitation range from "The Twist," a dance popularized by Chubby Checker, to the "Ali Shuffle," a professional fitness training exercise. I learned this particular Washing Machine Exercise from an Insight Meditation Center yoga teacher who shared it with our group. In my experience, this version of the Washing Machine Exercise works well in the classroom setting. I find it to be particularly effective when the kids are full of Tiger Energy and can't seem to settle down. Don't be surprised if the students feel calmer after this intense exercise.

EXERCISE: THE WASHING MACHINE

Begin by telling the students, "We're going to practice being washing machines." Standing up with feet planted about hip-wide, instruct them to begin by turning their torsos as far to the right as they can, using a swinging motion with their arms flung out and loose. As they do, make the sound "Cha." (This syllable is pronounced "sha" and it should be short, as in the "ah" of "Alleluia.") Next, tell them to swing around left in the same manner, once again, making the "Cha" sound. Lead the students in repeating this back-and-forth motion, gradually speeding up the swinging. From this point, proceed with the exercise in whatever manner suits your situation best. You may choose to use this swinging motion throughout the exercise, try one of the variations described below, or use your creativity as a teacher, experimenting with different washing machine "cycles" and "settings." In one possible variation, similar to the swinging at the beginning of the exercise, you can instruct the students to bend their arms in, chest high, and swing back and forth as fast as they can, shortening their turns. In another variation, you can tell students to bend and unbend their knees repeatedly, mimicking the center piece of a washing machine that moves up and down. At the end of the exercise, a spin cycle makes a great finale.

The next exercise is a rhythm game that I learned from a physical education teacher at Parker. It is great indoors (or out,) which makes it ideal for allowing movement on a rainy day.

EXERCISE: SECRET LEADER

To begin the game, a student is selected to leave the room, and then a "Secret Leader" is chosen. The leader creates a rhythm, and then the whole group joins in. The rhythm might be hand clapping, snapping fingers, floor slapping, or keeping a beat on knees or other body parts in a particular pattern. Once the group has joined in the rhythm, the student who left the room comes back into the circle, starts participating in the rhythm, and then guesses who started the rhythm. Finally, the "Secret Leader" is revealed. Then, if you like, a new student leaves the room, a new "Secret Leader" is selected, and the game begins again. I like a variation of this game in which two students are selected to leave the room together and then work together on figuring out who the "Secret Leader" is; this way no one feels like the worst or the best at the game.

Simple hand/brain teasers work well, also, when movement is called for in a class situation. Try to extend the thumb of your left hand and simultaneously point your index finger up. Now switch! HA!

You can have kids hold an ankle of one leg behind them, balance and then slowly bend down to touch their toes. There is a whole series of Tai Chi warmup exercises that are fabulous as de-stressors and for getting the *chi* flowing. Any hands on project can be used as a contemplative exercise, as has been identified in the previous chapters on the drawing of a labyrinth, for example.

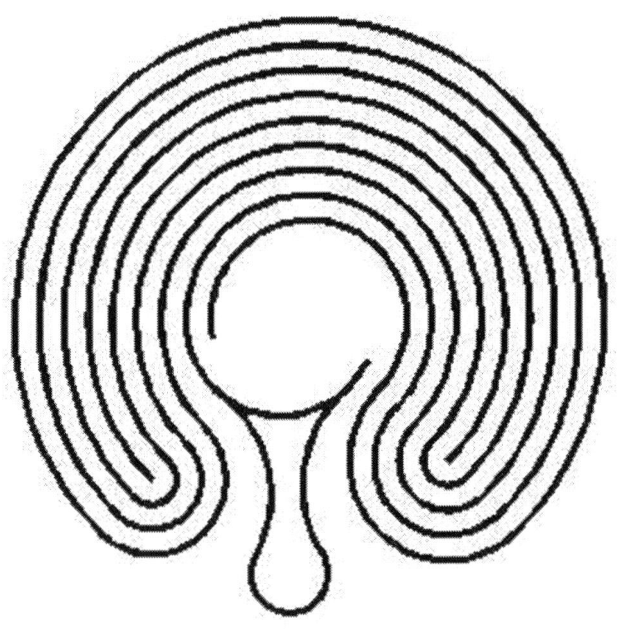

Labyrinths have a wonderful history, symbolizing the journey of life, representing switchbacks as the challenges and/or setbacks we encounter. Labyrinths can be relevant to math, history, architecture and the narrative journey in literature. (http://www.lessons4living.com/labyrinth.htm)

If your class is lucky enough to get permission to walk a real labyrinth, the experience could be utilized to represent their transition from one stage to another, a rite of passage, for example, from middle to high school or "tween" to teen. It is well known that when kids get their driver's licenses, they feel empowered as new adults. Any public and positive social ceremony that welcomes kids into a new level of responsibility and recognition for an accomplishment supports a positive identity. I suspect strongly that the temptation to rebel in dangerous ways might be mitigated if there were challenges and rituals that celebrated the new-found powers of youth.

During a weekend retreat, our former philosophy head had the group follow a ritual like the hero's journey where we were asked at the beginning, "What do you fear? What are your comforts? What do you most want?" I picked up a soft little bit of velvety green moss and wrapped it in a tissue "blanket" to symbolize my desire for "comfort." Others picked up various items as symbols of the fear of isolation or disease and brought them into a meeting with the leader. After we were interviewed and welcomed at the end of our journey, we celebrated with wine and cake.

A drama like this one doesn't need to be elaborately staged. Students could, in a single afternoon, place vinyl squares or mark off with masking tape a path in the gym or a basketball court, participate in the journey and receive some sort of little gift at the end. I had glass beads in reserve or smooth rocks as "prizes."

Alan Watts produced a little video years ago about how, as students, we are given the impression that life is a series of gates or goals where we are never satisfied, never can rest, and never feel as if we have achieved contentment or resolution. Students are told that they must study hard, get good grades, get into the best program, get their high school certificate, go to the best college, get their B.A., earn a Masters, marry the right person, join the country club, buy a big house, become a Rotarian.

Just writing the list is exhausting. Mr. Watts pointed out that life is not a journey with gates into bigger and better jobs: rather it is more like a symphony with beginnings and dramas and quiet interludes, harmonious times and cacophonies. If a person is so focused on a destination, how does one enjoy the present? The person keeps saying to themselves, "I'm not there yet." It is better to enjoy the times when you are pouring energy into a new project or just looking at the view. This amounts to accepting the stage of life you are currently in. What a joy to just be happy with no further requirements. Just to be.

CHAPTER 27

PICK UP THE PACE

Not every practice is designed to make people slow down. Going too slowly sometimes increases the opportunity for *Manas*, inner chatter and daydreaming, so you may want some ideas for energizing the kids who are half asleep. You can use this exercise to "Pick Up the Pace" in whatever way works best in your classroom.

The following list is comprised of activities you might instruct your students to do quickly and precisely. Tell the kids to focus their attention and to work as efficiently as possible.

- Math speed drills
- Spelling speed drills (common words)
- Typing drills
- Taking dictation
- Speed reading followed by comprehension questions

- Days of the week/ months of the year
- Length and volume drills (e.g. how many inches in a foot)
- Creating 10-item categorical lists (e.g. 10 vegetables, 10 cars, 10 trees)
- Matching games from lists of homophones, synonyms, or antonyms
- Puzzles
- Knitting, crocheting, beading
- Walking fast
- Cleaning or dusting the room
- Sorting games with objects (e.g. pencils, pens, beads, beans)

Anytime you find yourself or the students taking much too long doing a task, the chances are high that they are either adding unnecessary movements or daydreaming between actions. You can usually ask a class that is full of Sloth Energy to pick up the pace, and they will recognize the need for it. To signal a change like that you might say "Let's double the Pace."

These practices get their power through the concentration of energy along with a reduction of extraneous thoughts and movement. And some of these activities even provide the added benefit of a clean classroom!

CHAPTER 28

FOOD

A custom at the Advaita Meditation Center is that no one eats until everyone is served. It is civil custom for the teacher to make sure that each child has a full plate before anyone takes a bite. That way, the group is the central focus and concern. As a classroom practice, this can be required whenever there is a snack or meal. The entire group politely waits for everyone, asking what others would like and not serving themselves before anyone begins to eat. The reason is illustrated by the following story.

The well-known "Allegory of the Long Spoon," adapted by many traditions and religions including Jewish, Hindu, Buddhist, Oriental, and Christian, tells the story of a man who asked what the difference was between heaven and hell. He was told that in hell, all the people sit along both sides of long banquet tables where scrumptious soup is served, but they are starving because their wooden spoons have handles that are too long and they cannot reach their own mouths and feed themselves. Then the man was told that in heaven, like in hell, all the people sit along both sides of long banquet tables where scrumptious soup is served, and also, like in hell, they are all holding long-handled spoons and cannot feed themselves. However, in heaven, each person uses his/her spoon to feed the person across from them at the banquet table, and they all enjoy the scrumptious meal.

Mrs. Grigg, wife of the former principal of the Philosophy Foundation and a wise woman, once told me that in order to stop yourself from being poisoned, all you have to do is "taste" your food. I think she meant that we would not be inclined to eat foods that are "not so good" for us if we were aware of their taste instead of just gulping everything down. For example, many candies are sweet, which is pleasant at first, but there is often a chemical aftertaste and the sweetness can be a little nauseating. If we get used to the chemical aftertaste or over-sweet taste, our ability to perceive natural taste will become diminished. For example, carrots are sweet, but few people experience them as sweet. Younger people have a better sense of taste than adults do, but our junk food culture ruins what otherwise might be healthy perception!

The purpose of this Food Textures exercise is to have kids become more aware of their sense of taste, feel the textures in the mouth, and thoughtfully consider the effect these foods might have on the body.

EXERCISE: THE FLAVOR OF FOOD

For this activity, you will need a variety of food choices in the form of little curls or maybe some "slush" created by the food processor; it is important that the type of food cannot be identified by its texture. Some of the food choices that may work are: raw potatoes, radish, carrot, celery, ginger, beet, avocado, lettuce, mint, parsnips, apple, and so on. I do not recommend something that kids *want* to dive into, such as pretzels or chocolate.

Set up several stations around the classroom featuring one food each. Make sure to present the food in such a way that students will be able to feed each other while remaining sanitary and safe. For example, you might need toothpicks or "popsicle" sticks. Also include paper and pencils for making observations at each station. Instruct the students to partner up. As the pairs visit each station, the first partner is blindfolded and the second partner feeds the first partner and writes down their comments. Have the students visit each station, and tell the kids to take turns tasting and feeding/observing. Ask them to determine and decide if they think the food would produce Tiger, Swan, or Sloth energy, or if the food seems wholesome and nourishing, and any other comments. Collect the "comment" papers and share your observations.

The Lemon Exercise is a good get-to-know-you exercise or end-of-year de-stressor. Preferably it's done on a hot day, when everyone can enjoy a glass of cold lemonade after the practice. This exercise develops visual perceptions, writing skills and social interactions.

THE LEMON EXERCISE

For this exercise, you will need one lemon for each pair of students. To set up the activity, put the pile of lemons on one side of a table and set out some paper and pencils on the other side of the table. Tell the students to partner up and send a representative from each pair to get a lemon, paper, and pencil. Send the kids off to examine their lemon very carefully, noticing all the bumps, black spots, green squiggles, lumps, and so on. Ask them to write down a detailed description of their lemon. Next, instruct the students to return their lemons to the appropriate side of the table and their papers to the other side of the table. When all the lemons and descriptions are turned in, mix up the lemons and shuffle the papers.

Tell the pairs to first choose a paper, making sure that it's not their own, and second, visit the mixed-up lemon pile to find the lemon described in the paper they picked up. After each description is matched to the correct lemon, place the lemon on top of the proper description. Share observations with the whole group, and then enjoy a glass of lemonade.

III

SOCIAL SKILLS

CHAPTER 29

SOCIAL CAPITAL

Social capital is defined as the amount of respect, recognition, admiration and acceptance that you get from your peers. People who are charismatic leaders have a great deal of social capital. Even when they commit crimes or get caught red-handed doing something wrong, they are so charming that they are often forgiven. The young people who have a great deal of this commodity need to be taught to be kind and generous about extending their circle to include those with fewer gifts. They are "pupular," my son would say.

A Stanford professor who has been studying wild chimpanzees for years says that dominance and the privileges of dominance actually change the brain's chemistry. There are equivalent brain changes to those activated by stress or being the recipient of harassment from authority. It is nearly certain that some kids will be on the receiving end of negative aspects of group dynamics.

People who may be socially awkward, shy, the family scapegoat, or the butt of put-downs in school are not doing anything intentionally being the way they are. Often, people with low social capital have learning disabilities, do not read social situations well, or are the smallest or youngest in a given group. Sometimes buckteeth, crossed eyes or certain physical disabilities contribute to low social capital. Long after the physical problem is gone, the residue from this period remains. Once life puts a person in a disadvantaged situation, it is not only the person's reactions, but also the situations and attitudes of others that create perception and subsequent defense mechanisms.

The principal of the old Philosophy Foundation, Mr. Cedric Grigg, once told me that the most certain way of "killing" someone was to form an opinion of him or her and refuse to change it. Once a reputation is established, the biases towards those individuals are very hard to undo. The most damaging part is that the individual who is "thought" of in a certain way often finds herself being constantly defensive against these attitudes or accepting them as true, internalizing them, and thereby becoming what people think of her. Toxic shame constrains the heart and creates a defensive posture in kids. It needs to be gently lifted so that the students feel comfortable exposing their weaknesses and gaps in learning. It is only when a child trusts you enough to ask their questions, can you really help.

Students with learning disabilities are often told that they're not trying, they're lazy and/or stupid, they're upsetting or shaming their parents, they're not like their brother, etc. A cycle begins where sincere improvement attempts end in humiliation and failure. The child begins to resist and resent any attempts to "teach" him/her. It might be helpful if teachers assume that kids are actually doing the best they know how or that if they are struggling and resentful, they have good reasons to be that way.

So how does a teacher ease the hurt and constraint from past social and educational traumas? By sitting quietly with a child, you can often figure out what sort of impediment is holding back his learning. Ask the child to describe what he is thinking as he does an assignment. Listen carefully to what is said and how the processes are described. If the child uses words having to do with a certain sense, such as "Oh now I see what you mean," or "Finally I can hear what you are saying," you can determine that their dominant learning style is seeing, hearing or some other sense. On the other hand, a "Learning Style" preference is less of a hindrance than a learning disability. Because this question is so complex and a science in itself, I will leave that to the specialists in your school. (See LDonline.com or the National Center for Learning Disabilities at http://www.ncld.org/ for additional information.) Even after gathering the data and recommendations from the specialists, and by working quietly with the children, you can usually intuit how to meet their needs. I often feel some kind of tug in my heart that gives me a sense of what they are thinking. This information depends on your receptivity. You may pick up how a child perceives and processes information but it is more important that the child trusts you than any special technique or machine.

A child who lacks social capital needs your support and kindness. They are the ones who suffer the most from a nearly inescapable amount of stress — and even bullying –in the middle and high school years. You can,

Focus on Students

Kids on the autism scale do not "fake" a polite interest in others, even though it would be expected in "normal" conversation. At the Parker school, *advisory* was a time to talk. In the mornings, "statements" were made about what was important to each student, and in the afternoon, they reviewed and reflected on their day. In the 7th grade, the statements were often the verbal equivalent of parallel play, but as the student gets older, she/he connects and reflects more on other's ideas.

When a kid is perceived as not picking up social cues, it helps for the teacher to give them some stock supportive phrases such as, "Wow, that must have been hard" or "Good for you!" to enhance their acceptance in the group.

however, teach kids who have these challenges a number of strategies that will make their lives easier. One method is for the student to work with younger children as a tutor, teacher, or service person. The younger children almost always admire older ones; their status automatically becomes positive, whether or not they have social capital within their peer group. If you think that is a suitable route, it's a way for awkward students to gain skills and respect. Nothing teaches like the experience of teaching.

Another option is to give students a chance to share a special talent or 'hobby" with others. Clubs and after school activities often function as a way to bring status to kids who may not shine in the academic classroom. As a teacher, you can look for opportunities to "coach" an awkward child to find ways to showcase their special talents. You can encourage them to join groups of students who have similar interests and support their growth by letting them lead an activity which they are able to execute well.

In addition to teaching students who have weak social skills how to cope better, you can also teach the group to have more understanding and compassion for people they usually avoid. Children often don't have the language to describe how they feel, and they may not recognize that a physical feeling, emotional distress and perceptions are intimately connected.

A frequent theme in all sorts of guided meditations is aspects of healing and safety. The following script is designed to soften the hard edges of social judgment, help students feel better, and encourage the kids to be mindful and allow the *chi*, the energy of the universe, to correct any imbalance that might exist.

MAGIC POTION

After a Stop, read the following script to the students:

Close your eyes and visualize your very favorite color, and place that color with your mind about 15 inches away from your nose. Take a few deep breaths, and with each breath, energize that color so that it sparkles, bubbles and shines in the light.

Imagine, now, that you can put that sparkling liquid into a vial or tube of some kind. Next, choose your very favorite flavor. It can be anything you like, peppermint or root beer or pomegranate, for example. Flavor your sparkling liquid with this ingredient.

Now gently reach out for your magic potion. Sip it. It tastes wonderful. As it goes down, and you notice that it seems to fix things just exactly as needed. If you are tired, it soothes. If you are dull, it enlivens. If you feel sad, it adds cheer. If you are worried, it provides calm. This energy knows you and provides exactly what you need, in just the right way.

Now rest with this for a little while.

As a follow-up activity, specifically for those students who are more confident and who have good social capital, the next exercise will get them thinking about compassion:

DEVELOPING COMPASSION

Close your eyes and imagine your very best friend. Think about the good times you have had together. Now think about the talents and qualities of your best friend that you admire. They might be boldness, honesty, humor, creativity, and loyalty. Allow their good qualities to emerge in your mind; understand that these are the reasons why you like spending time with this friend.

Now think about another person you normally avoid. Imagine your friend talking to that person and bringing them into your circle of friends. Your best friend tells you that this person has one or two outstanding qualities. What do you know them to be?

Consider how those qualities or talents are good, clever or useful. In your mind, tell that person that it's good that they can ....(fill in the talent, skill or trait). Thank them for doing that.

Return to room awareness and rest. Make an effort this week to think of this person in a new way. You might even make an effort to speak to her/him.

The following script is designed to help children who suffer from anxiety. It helps them to calm down by imaging a house or a safe place in their minds. The characteristics of the safe place are supposed to help the child connect to a sense of protection and calm.

A SAFE PLACE

Create in your mind the kind of land and weather that you love most in the whole world. It might be a beach or mountain. It might be the desert or a log cabin in deep pine woods. It could be a tree house or a hobbit hole. Wherever you would like to build yourself a safe home, do that now in your mind. Now, give your home a material, shape and texture. It can be concrete, wood, stucco, tile, glass, metal and so on. Next, create a door and living space, move on and create a hearth or kitchen, the place to eat and cook. Now create a place to bathe, and then one in which to sleep. Place in your home windows or open places and all the things you love such as a big comfy couch, a computer, curtains, plants, perhaps some animal companions. Surround your home with the kind of rocks or a garden that you like. Now go into it and find a place to rest and sit quietly. Make sure you can look out through your window in the same way your eyes look out of your body. Stay there for a time and enjoy the protection and energy it gives you. Allow yourself to feel safe, free, and at home.

CHAPTER 30

ANGER MANAGEMENT

Anger arises in many circumstances: when we feel that our dignity has been offended, when our good idea is put down, when we desperately want something to go a certain way but it doesn't, etc. Anger arises when we are attached to a particular result and expect that that desire will be met. If we are in *moha* which indicates mental stupefaction, and we are are blocked, then rage or *krodha* arises. That kind of rage begins with a desperate need to control things that can't be control.

It is nearly impossible to be "reasonable" if one is terrifically angry, and the last thing one wants to hear is, "you don't have any reason to feel that way." Anger doesn't appear to turn off like a switch, but it can wind down.

During a rather heated discussion once, I got the image that being angry was like riding a large, unruly horse; it felt dangerous, a bit overwhelming, taking maximum technique and self-control. It felt like the reins were the control of reason, but they were not quite getting through to this massive animal beneath me. I felt bucked and swayed by the sheer power of the emotion, but I wanted desperately to steer and subdue it.

In order to give kids a sense that they have some power over this upsurge of energy and feelings, you first need to acknowledge what they feel, why they feel it and that it is their reality, their reaction. Phrases that are supportive but neutral can help, such as: "That really bothered you, tell me more about it." Or, "oh I can see why you might be upset about that." These are more helpful than, "You have no reason to be that aggravated," or "Just Calm Down." For example, a child may be being truly and unjustly treated, so it important that you let them know you will do something about it. Adults have to stop bullies in school because the kids either cannot or will not.

Unfortunately, we cannot be responsible for the "perception" of others, but we can avoid provocation in careful, thoughtful ways. I will admit that I myself have never been successful at predicting what would distress others and have gotten myself into hot water frequently.

If you have to get close to a child who is about to explode, it is a good idea to keep your hands visible, crouch, sit or kneel and speak softly. If you try to intimidate or loom over them, their defensiveness may increase. I like providing a corner of the class as the "chill" corner. It is designed to reduce stress by having pillows, a coffee table, a screen, book shelf or whatever, to increase a sense of protection. It is NOT the teacher's job to process emotions; that is what school counselors are trained to do. This is just a temporary holding space.

Nevertheless, anything you can do to slow down, create space away from the incident and the stimulus of the reaction is what is important. If the child can, in any way, detach from the specifics of the incident and begin to see both sides of the issues or the incident in context of a larger time period, it will turn the desperate feeling of being badly treated to a more moderate "live and let live" attitude.

ANGER MANAGEMENT EXERCISE:

As a calming exercise you may have them write the answers to

- What happened?
- What should have happened?
- Why did it happen?
- What can you do about it now?

As they write their thoughts, their energy is being directed into a description, and, generally, after the twenty minutes it takes to write and review it, the student is more under control.

You may also encourage them to "cool" off by thinking about anger as a liquid ball of metal. Here is the exercise:

MY FIRE BECOMES STEEL

Ask them to get a big glass of cold water. As they drink the water, have them tell themselves the water is cooling off the anger. Anger is like molten metal; as it cools, it becomes steel. Steel is stronger than liquid. It is solid and steady. They can stand strong in their "steel self" rather than lashing out. They are sturdy, solid, heavy, powerful, and immune to being annoyed or pushed about by temporary situations. This steel self is a ball that rolls easily and does not get stuck or caught. It has no edges so there nothing for people to hold on to.

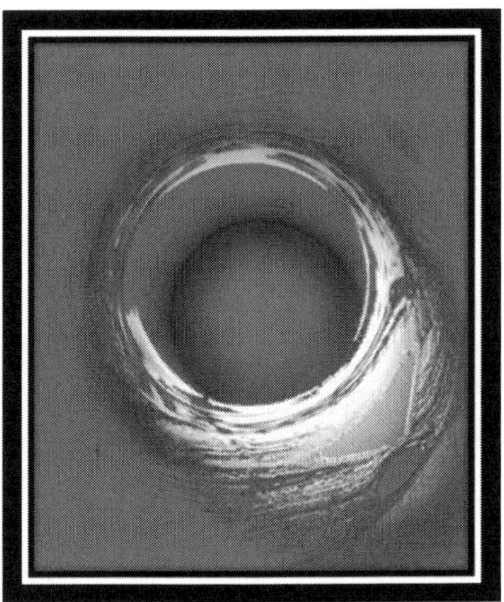

CHAPTER 31

10 SIMPLE PRACTICES

When I am having an especially dopey day (I call them Jell-O days where my mind simply will not function), I try to think of a rule to practice that will help. A person can practice any one of these rules which may prevent a whole lot of grief. So the addendum to this list is: **if you haven't a clue, a rule will do!**

Each one of these little exercises can be taught as the practice for the week or the day. It is not the length of time that one knows about mindfulness that has an effect on the being, it is the sincerity and number of times a person actually practices that makes all the difference. All of the practices depend on the depth of your own practice.

1. Come to a complete rest before beginning a new task
2. Do one thing at a time
3. Complete each action
4. Focus the attention where the work is taking place
5. Don't criticize yourself or others
6. Do what is needed without regard for likes and dislikes
7. Create a quiet, clean environment
8. Consider one another
9. Work for improvement, not perfection
10. Create helpful routines: study, rest, play and work in the proper amounts each day.

Here is a list to refer to frequently that is based on Vedanta and the methods used to raise awareness for people who attend the Advaita Meditation Center. The master practice is, of course, meditation from which the strength to remember comes.

Any activity can become a contemplative exercise, and the different practices shown above can help to change the focus just enough to keep it interesting. When a class is asked to do a hands-on project, you can say: "listen to the sound where the working surfaces meet" or "watch your hands as you work." Any physical task can be used as a meditation, especially projects such as building a boat, a model, gardening, washing dishes and so on. Watching your hands at work is advocated in this Sanskrit *shruti* with the following words:

"Where the hand goes, the eye goes

Where the eye goes, there the mind follows

Where the mind is, there the heart is also

Where the heart is, there love arises." (Nandikesvara - Abhinayadarpanam)

Do one thing at a time is one of the exercises. This may seem easy, but it essential to being on task, open to the present moment and receptive to the information nature is providing us right now. Most of the time, we are thinking, and in that "dream," we believe we are being attentive. However, if the mind is making comments or subtly shifting from liking to disliking the task, these will actually block your availability to attend.

Try a simple task such as chopping carrots. As you place the knife against the skin of the carrot, what really happens? How does the carrot feel in your fingers? Does the carrot snap or do the cells part when the blade touches them? Is there a sound? How much pressure is needed? Where does the sound come from, the carrot or the bottom when you contact the surface of the board?

When we are really challenged by a task and go deeply into it, we are able to solve problems and recognize appropriate strategies with sustained concentration. I am reminded of Ray Bradbury's classic short story, "I sing the body Electric," where the Grandmother says, "**If paying attention is love, I am love.**"

SANSKRIT GLOSSARY

antakarana	habitual emotions and ideas, the sum of the mental and emotional setup
agni	fire, one of the material elements
akasha	ether, the least dense of material substances, transmits sound
ananda	happiness, contentment
anhankara	a collection of our ideas about ourselves, ego
Atmana	the self within
bhumi	earth- tiny particles that create earth
buddhi	discrimination, allows the mind to tell real from unreal
chit	consciouness
chitta	the organ of the mind that carries love or other emotions.
krodha	anger triggered by frustrated attachment, rage
darma	good works
ekagra	one pointed attention
gunas	the great states of energy
guru	teacher, means "heavy"
japa	repetition of matramantra quickly
Jnana	wisdom
karma	the consequence of an action
kshipta	distraction, attention divided
manas	discursive mind, head chatter, memory or imagination
mantra	a sacred word, often one of the names of God
pancha bhuuta	five elements of ether, air, fire, water and earth
prana	breath
rajas	the guna of passion, energy
samskara	situations in life that appear to be challenges created by the past (incarnations)

sat	consciousness, purity
satchitanada	truth, consciousness, bliss
satva	the guna of consciousness, purity,
tamas	ignorance, sleep, dullness, crystallized form
titiksha	restraint, staying focused in spite of distractions bearing with equanimity the pairs of opposites, heat and cold, pleasure and pain, and respectful and disrespectful treatment; endurance.
vayu	water
vedanata	the way
viveka	discrimination between the finite/infinite, real, unreal
yoga	union

All of the Artwork in this book has been created by my talented husband, Ken Gidge, the creative force behind 3D paintings and these digital images. These pictures are the black and white versions of his brilliantly colored art work seen at GidgeWorld.com.

AFTERTHOUGHT: WHY WE DO THIS AUGUST 2013

Unlike numbers, if you complete seven practices that ought to make you kind, generous, attentive, sleeping and eating well, meditating, and exercising, you are not guaranteed an unchallenged life. These practices lead to some resilience, better stress management and some guidance about how to make good choices. There is, however, no magic wand that makes the tools work like a mathematical equation because, essentially, all of this is based on service to others. Happiness is ungraspable; it arises when you share and are open to the wonder of this creation. However, if you do use the practices, you will make positive improvements in your life. Other people may notice before you do than you can study longer, are more patient and are less likely to take a bad mood out on others.

With regard to your students, one of my mentors who had taught middle school for 30 years, said, "This is the time that the students make the moral decision to be good or evil." Their budding awareness of the world invites a consideration of whether they will try to help and contribute to the world or to take something special for themselves with no consideration for anyone else. It is the basic choice all humans have to make: "Will I give back to creation what I have been given? Or will I be a thief?" Generally, the more nourished and aware the child is, the more inclined s/he is to appreciate the abundance of this world. As Jesus instructed in the parable of the talents, we must take the talents given to us and increase them.

So, good luck with this very tough audience! The results of your work may not be seen until years later when a college student comes back and says to you, "You know that thing you taught me, it really helps." Namaste, Lee Guerette

REFERENCES

Antonov, Vladimir, Ph.D., editor, "Selected Excerpts from the Bhagavad Gita" (2010) in the *Encyclopedia of Spiritual Knowledge*, Retrieved from: http://www.encyclopedia-of-religion.org/guna.html

Chan, Philip A. and Terry Rabinowitz. "A cross-sectional analysis of video games and attention deficit hyperactivity disorder symptoms in adolescents." *Annuls of General Psychiatry.* 2006; 5: 16. Published online 2006 October 24. 10.1186/1744-859X-5-1

"Elements of Vastu Shastra." (n.d.) In *Vaastu Shastra: the Encyclopedia on Vastu Shastra.* Retrieved from http://www.vaastu-shastra.com/elements-of-vastu-shastra.html

Flook, Lisa, et al. "Effects of Mindful Awareness Practices on Executive Function in Elementary School Children." *Journal of Applied School Psychology* 26: 70-95.ISSN 1537-7903 print/1537-7911 online (2010): 70-95. Print.

Kurtz, Lisa A. *Understanding Motor Skills in Children with Dyspraxia, ADHD, Autism, and Other Learning Disabilities: A Guide to Improving Coordination.* Jessica Kingsley Publishers, 2007. Google eBook.

Lehrer, J. (2011, January 19). "The Neuroscience of Music" [Web log comment]. Retrieved from http://www.wired.com/wiredscience/2011/01/the-neuroscience-of-music

Morales, F.M. (2003). "The Three Gunas: The metaphysical grounding of physical reality." Retrieved from http://www.veda-academy.com/articles/vedanta/three_gunas.htm

Paramanada, Swami, *Silence as Yoga*. Cohasset, Mass: Vedanta Center publishers, 1974. Print.

Rozman, Deborah. *Meditating with Children – The Art of Concentrating and Centering: A Workbook on New Educational Methods Using Meditation.* Integral Yoga Editions. (1975, Revised Edition, 2002)

Steinberg, Scott, *The Modern Parents' Guide to Kids and Video Games,* Power Play Publishing, 2011

Yoo, H.J., S.C. Choo, S.K. Yune, S.K. Kim, "Attention deficit hyperactivity syndromes and internet addiction." Psychiatry and Clinical

WHY COGNITIVE YOGA NOW?

Congress has mandated that all public schools teach Social Emotional learning by 2016.

The Mindfulness in Education movement is cutting edge in innovations right now.

Middle School kids need short, interesting practices that are adjusted to their stage of development. There are only a handful of books for this age group.

My source is Advaita Vedanta which is acknowledged as an authoritative source for understanding how the mind works. The teacher may share as much or as little as they wish of Vedanta.

This book is a combination of techniques that work well with typical students and special needs students based on years of work with both.

Instead of approaching behavior control from the outside–in, from the teacher intimidating the students with threats of detention or calling parents, this is control through the student's willingness to engage in effective and productive behavior for themselves.

The pauses, guided imagination and practical exercises help kids develop critical thinking skills. Shallow thinking and passive learning styles, sometimes attributed to the constant stream of entertainment, is at an all-time high, and teachers are desperate for an antidote.

Author's Credentials

MA Reading and Language, Boston University

BA English Literature

Teacher Certification in
Reading & Learning Disabilities Mass/N.H.
Accredited to award PDPS in Massachusetts by the Department of Education

30 years as a member of the Advaita Meditation Center

Trained in the .B program:
Six Seconds Teacher Training

Member of the Mindfulness in Education Group

SEL4Mass member
Certified Six Second Educator/Coach

EQ Educators Network

Ten percent of the proceeds from the sale of this book will be donated to the Advaita Meditation Center or to some other charitable institution that supports teachers.

The techniques presented in Cognitive Yoga have been used for a decade. My intended audience is middle school teachers who are interested in using mindfulness in the classroom. Students in this age group can be especially challenging because they bring their strong opinions to the table and are in a stage of great growth. The work is presented to you in the hopes that it will help you in two important ways. First, it will make your life as a teacher easier. Second, as you instruct using the techniques described in this book, your students will benefit by learning methods that will help them be aware of their ideas and emotions, increase empathy for other students, and improve their ability to focus on their work.

Mentoring Teachers

Mindful activities are challenging to teach. It requires deep self-examination, the ability to be ready for anything that arises in the classroom, and a peaceful demeanor right down to your toenails. I offer coaching in mindfulness to teachers who are introducing these practices into their own classroom. This kind of collaboration will provide you with empathetic support to sustain and encourage you. Write to Leeguerette@gmail.com or call: **603-888-2355.**

www.cognitiveyoga.com website and blog https://www.facebook.com/CognitiveYoga

Available to run .B courses, an introduction to Mindfulness on site for students in the 7th – 9th grades

Free Introductory lecture, consultation, workshops, presenter for conferences, professional development courses

Available per Diem

Availability

Lee Guerette is available to teach how to use Emotional Intelligence to create a great learning environment. Giving teacher tools to weave the benefits of Social Emotional learning into the classroom. Teaching students to manage their attention and energy, promote collaboration, communication, goal setting and executive function. Practical exercises that enhance learning and promote critical thinking.

- SEL increases academic achievement by 11%,
- Teachers with SEL skills have better management of classes and better relationships with their students
- SEL reduces the incidents and the costs of disciplinary interventions
- Understanding how to focus, collaborate and manage emotions is a life skill
- SEL supports resilience, creativity, and critical thinking
- SEL counteracts teacher burnout